About the author

David Butt

David Butt (b.1950) tutored in Linguistics at Macquarie University from 1978 to 1983. Originally a student of English literature and language (from the University of New South Wales), David took up a Postgraduate Research Scholarship at Macquarie in order to study textlinguistics. His doctoral thesis, 'The relationship between theme and lexico-grammar in the poetry of Wallace Stevens' argued for the central role of linguistics in the study of literature. The study used systemic-functional linguistics to demonstrate the semantic consequences of textual patterning in Stevens's work.

After completing his doctorate, he spent two years at the National University of Singapore, where he lectured in the School of English Language and Literature from 1986–87.

Currently David is a Lecturer in Linguistics at Macquarie University, Sydney.

He is married with two children.

Paull Mayne and David have known each other since infants' school at Manly, New South Wales. Paull also attended the University of New South Wales where he majored in Psychology and English. He has taught at secondary schools, including a school for students who have difficulty adapting to a school environment. He holds a Master's degree in counselling at Macquarie University, and works as a school counsellor in Sydney.

Talking and thinking: the patterns of behaviour

David Butt

Series Editor: Frances Christie

Oxford University Press
1989

Oxford University Press
Walton Street, Oxford OX2 6DP

Oxford   New York   Toronto
Delhi   Bombay   Calcutta   Madras   Karachi
Petaling Jaya   Singapore   Hong Kong   Tokyo
Nairobi   Dar es Salaam   Cape Town
Melbourne   Auckland

and associated companies in
Berlin   Ibadan

Oxford English and the *Oxford English* logo are trade marks of
Oxford University Press

ISBN 019 437151 4

Printed in Hong Kong.

Foreword

In a sense, educational interest in language is not new. Studies of rhetoric and of grammar go back as far as the Greeks; in the English-speaking countries, studies of the classical languages, and more recently of English itself, have had a well established place in educational practice. Moreover, a number of the issues which have aroused the most passionate debates about how to develop language abilities have tended to remain, resurfacing at various points in history in somewhat different formulations perhaps, but nonetheless still there, and still lively.

Of these issues, probably the most lively has been that concerning the extent to which explicit knowledge about language on the part of the learner is a desirable or a useful thing. But the manner in which discussion about this issue has been conducted has often been allowed to obscure other and bigger questions: questions, for example, both about the nature of language as an aspect of human experience, and about language as a resource of fundamental importance in the building of human experience. The tendency in much of the western intellectual tradition has been to dissociate language and experience, in such a way that language is seen as rather neutral, merely serving to 'carry' the fruits of experience. Whereas in this view language is seen as a kind of 'conduit', subservient to experience in various ways, an alternative view, as propounded in the books in this series, would argue that language is itself not only a part of experience, but intimately involved in the manner in which we construct and organise experience. As such, it is never neutral, but deeply implicated in building meaning. One's notions concerning how to teach about language will differ quite markedly, depending upon the view one adopts concerning language and experience. In fact, though discussions concerning teaching about language can sometimes be interesting, in practice many such discussions have proved theoretically ill-founded and barren, serving merely to perpetuate a number of unhelpful myths about language.

The most serious and confusing of these myths are those which would suggest we can dissociate language from meaning — form from function, or form from 'content'. Where such myths apply, teaching about language becomes a matter of teaching about 'language rules' — normally grammatical rules — and as history has demonstrated over the years, such teaching rapidly degenerates into the arid pursuit of parts of speech and the parsing of isolated sentences. Meaning, and the critical role of language in the building of meaning, are simply overlooked, and the kinds of knowledge about language made available to the learner are of a very limited kind.

The volumes in this series of monographs devoted to language education in my view provide a much better basis upon which to address questions related to the teaching about language than has been the case anywhere in the English-speaking world for some time now. I make this claim for several reasons, one of the most important being that the series never sought directly to establish a model for teaching about language at all. On the contrary, it sought to establish a principled model of language, which, once properly articulated, allows us to address many questions of an educational nature, including those to do with teaching about language. To use Halliday's term (1978), such a model sees language primarily as a 'social semiotic', and as a resource for meaning, centrally involved in the processes by which human beings negotiate, construct and change the nature of social experience. While the series certainly does not claim to have had the last word on these and related subjects, I believe it does do much to set a new educational agenda — one which enables us to look closely at the role of language both in living and in learning: one which, moreover, provides a basis upon which to decide those kinds of teaching and learning about language which may make a legitimate contribution to the development of the learner.

I have said that arguments to do with teaching about language have been around for a long time: certainly as long as the two hundred years of white settlement in Australia. In fact, coincidentally, just as the first settlers were taking up their enforced residence in the Australian colony of New South Wales, Lindley Murray was preparing his *English Grammar* (1795), which, though not the only volume produced on the subject in the eighteenth century, was certainly the best. Hundreds of school grammars that were to appear in Britain and Australia for the next century at least, were to draw very heavily upon what Murray had written. The parts of speech, parsing and sentence analysis, the latter as propounded by Morell (an influential inspector of schools in England), were the principal elements in the teaching about language in the Australian colonies, much as they were in England throughout the century. By the 1860s and 1870s the Professor of Classics and Logic at Sydney University, Charles Badham, who had arrived from England in 1867, publicly disagreed with the examining authorities in New South Wales concerning the teaching of grammar. To the contemporary reader there is a surprising modernity about many of his objections, most notably his strongly held conviction that successful control of one's language is learned less as a matter of committing to memory the parts of speech and the principles of parsing, than as a matter of frequent opportunity for use.

Historically, the study by which issues of use had been most effectively addressed had been that of rhetoric, in itself quite old in the English-speaking tradition, dating back at least to the sixteenth century. Rhetorical studies flourished in the eighteenth century, the best known works on the subject being George Campbell's *The Philosophy of Rhetoric* (1776), and Hugh Blair's *Lectures on Rhetoric and Belles Lettres* (1783), while in the nineteenth century Richard Whately published his work, *Elements of Rhetoric* (1828). As the nineteenth century proceeded, scholarly work on rhetoric declined, as was testified by the markedly inferior but nonetheless influential works of Alexander Bain (*English Composition and Rhetoric*, 1866; Revised version, 1887). Bain, in fact, did much to corrupt and destroy the older rhetorical traditions, primarily because he lost sight of the need for a basic concern with meaning in language. Bain's was the century of romanticism after all: on the one hand, Matthew Arnold was extolling the civilising influence of English literature in the development of children; on the other hand, there was a tendency towards suspicion, even contempt, for those who wanted to take a scholarly look at the linguistic organisation of texts, and at the ways in which they were structured for the building of meaning. In 1921, Ballard (who was an expert witness before the Newbolt Enquiry on the teaching of English), wrote a book called *Teaching the Mother Tongue*, in which he noted among other things, that unfortunately in England at least rhetorical studies had become associated with what were thought to be rather shallow devices for persuasion and argument. The disinclination to take seriously the study of the rhetorical organisation of texts gave rise to a surprisingly unhelpful tradition for the teaching of literature, which is with us yet in many places: 'civilising' it might be, but it was *not* to be the object of systematic study, for such study would in some ill-defined way threaten or devalue the work of literature itself.

A grammarian like Murray had never been in doubt about the relationship of grammar and rhetoric. As he examined it, grammar was concerned with the syntax of the written English sentence: it was not concerned with the study of 'style', about which he wrote a short appendix in his original grammar, where his debt to the major rhetoricians of the period was apparent. Rhetorical studies, especially as discussed by Campbell for instance, did address questions of 'style', always from the standpoint of a recognition of the close relationship of language to the socially created purpose in using language. In fact, the general model of language as discussed by Campbell bore some relationship to the model taken up in this series, most notably in its commitment to register.

The notion of register proposes a very intimate relationship of text to context: indeed, so intimate is that relationship, it is asserted, that the one can only be interpreted by reference to the other. Meaning is realised in language (in the form of text), which is thus shaped or patterned in response to the context of situation in which it is used. To study language then, is to concentrate upon exploring how it is systematically patterned towards important social ends. The linguistic theory adopted here is that of systemic linguistics. Such a linguistic theory is itself also a social theory, for it proposes firstly, that it is in the nature of human behaviour to build reality and/or experience through complex semiotic processes, and secondly, that the principal semiotic system available to humans is their language. In this sense, to study language is to explore some of the most important and pervasive of the processes by which human beings build their world.

I originally developed the volumes in this series as the basis of two major off campus courses in Language Education taught in the Master's degree program at Deakin University, Victoria, Australia. To the best of my knowledge, such courses, which are designed primarily for teachers and teacher educators, are the first of their kind in the world, and while they actually appeared in the mid 1980s, they emerge from work in language education which has been going on in Australia for some time. This included the national Language Development Project, to which Michael Halliday was consultant, and whose work I co-ordinated throughout its second, productive phase. (This major project was initiated by the Commonwealth Government's Curriculum Development Centre, Canberra, in the 1970s, and involved the co-operation of curriculum development teams from all Australian states in developing language curriculum materials. Its work was not completed because of political changes which caused the activities of the Curriculum Development Centre to be wound down.) In the 1980s a number of conferences have been held fairly regularly in different parts of Australia, all of them variously exploring aspects of language education, and leading to the publication of a number of conference reports. They include: Frances Christie (ed.), *Language and the Social Construction of Experience* (Deakin University, 1983); Brendan Bartlett and John Carr (eds.), *Language in Education Workshop: a Report of Proceedings* (Centre for Research and Learning, Brisbane C.A.E., Mount Gravatt Campus, Brisbane, 1984); Ruqaiya Hasan (ed.), *Discourse on Discourse* (Applied Linguistics Association of Australia, Occasional Papers, Number 7, 1985); Clare Painter and J.R. Martin (eds.), *Writing to Mean: Teaching Genres across the Curriculum* (Applied Linguistics Association of Australia, Occasional Papers, Number 9, 1986); Linda Gerot, Jane Oldenburg and Theo Van Leeuwen (eds.), *Language and Socialisation: Home and School* (in preparation). All these activities have contributed to the building of a climate of opinion and a tradition of thinking about language which made possible the development of the volumes in this series.

While it is true that the developing tradition of language education which these volumes represent does, as I have noted, take up some of the concerns of the older rhetorical studies, it nonetheless also looks forward, pointing to ways of examining language which were not available in earlier times. For example, the notion of language as a social semiotic, and its associated conception of experience or reality as socially built and constantly subject to processes of transformation, finds very much better expression today than would have been possible before, though obviously much more requires to be said about this than can be dealt with in these volumes. In addition, a functionally driven view of language is now available, currently most completely articulated in Halliday's *An Introduction to Functional Grammar* (1985), which offers ways of understanding the English language in a manner that Murray's Grammar could not have done.

Murray's Grammar confined itself to considerations of the syntax of the written English sentence. It did not have anything of use to say about spoken language, as opposed to written language, and, equally, it provided no basis upon which to explore a unit other than the sentence, whether that be the paragraph, or, even more importantly, the total text. The preoccupation with the written sentence reflected the pre-eminent position being accorded to the written word by Murray's time, leading to disastrous consequences since, that is the diminished value accorded to spoken language, especially in educational practices. In Murray's work, the lack of a direct relationship between the study of grammar on the one hand, and that of 'style', on the other hand, was, as I have already noted, to be attributed to his view that it was the rhetorician who addressed wider questions relating to the text. In the tradition in which he worked, in fact, grammar looked at syntactic rules divorced from considerations of meaning or social purpose.

By contrast, Halliday's approach to grammar has a number of real strengths, the first of which is the fact that its basis is semantic, not syntactic: that is to say, it is a semantically driven grammar, which, while not denying that certain principles of syntax do apply, seeks to consider and identify the role of various linguistic items in any text in terms of their function in building meaning. It is for this reason that its practices for interpreting and labelling various linguistic items and groupings are functionally based, not syntactically based. There is in other words, no dissociation of 'grammar' on the one hand and 'semantics' or meaning on the other. A second strength of Halliday's approach is that it is not uniquely interested in written language, being instead committed to the study of both the spoken and written modes, and to an explanation of the differences between the two, in such a way that each is illuminated because of its contrast with the other. A third and final strength of the systemic functional grammar is that it permits useful movement across the text, addressing the manner in which linguistic patternings are built up for the construction of the overall text in its particular 'genre', shaped as it is in response to the context of situation which gave rise to it.

Halliday's functional grammar lies behind all ten volumes in this series, though one other volume, by Michael Christie, called *Aboriginal perspectives on experience and learning: the role of language in Aboriginal Education*, draws upon somewhat different if still compatible perspectives in educational and language theory to develop its arguments. The latter volume, is available directly from Deakin University. In varying ways, the volumes in this series provide a helpful introduction to much that is more fully dealt with in Halliday's Grammar, and I commend the series to the reader who wants to develop some sense of the ways such a body of linguistic theory can be applied to educational questions. A version of the grammar specifically designed for teacher education remains to be written, and while I cherish ambitions to begin work on such a version soon, I am aware that others have similar ambitions − in itself a most desirable development.

While I have just suggested that the reader who picks up any of the volumes in this series should find ways to apply systemic linguistic theory to educational theory, I want to argue, however, that what is offered here is more than merely a course in applied linguistics, legitimate though such a course might be. Rather, I want to claim that this is a course in educational linguistics, a term of importance because it places linguistic study firmly at the heart of educational enquiry. While it is true that a great deal of linguistic research of the past, where it did not interpret language in terms of interactive, social processes, or where it was not grounded in a concern for meaning, has had little of relevance to offer education, socially relevant traditions of linguistics like that from which systemics is derived, do have a lot to contribute. How that contribution should be articulated is quite properly a matter of development in partnership between educationists, teachers and linguistics, and a great deal has yet to be done to achieve such articulation.

I believe that work in Australia currently is making a major contribution to the development of a vigorous educational linguistics, not all of it of course in a systemic framework. I would note here the important work of such people as J.R. Martin, Joan Rothery, Suzanne Eggins and Peter Wignell of the University of Sydney, investigating children's writing development; the innovatory work of Brian Gray and his colleagues a few years ago in developing language programs for Aboriginal children in central Australia, and more recently his work with other groups in Canberra; the recent work of Beth Graham, Michael Christie and Stephen Harris, all of the Northern Territory Department of Education, in developing language programs for Aboriginal children; the important work of John Carr and his colleagues of the Queensland Department of Education in developing new perspectives upon language in the various language curriculum guidelines they have prepared for their state; the contributions of Jenny Hammond of the University of Wollongong, New South Wales, in her research into language development in schools, as well as the various programs in which she teaches; research being undertaken by Ruqaiya Hasan and Carmel Cloran of Macquarie University, Sydney, into children's language learning styles in the transition years from home to school; investigations by Linda Gerot, also of Macquarie University, into classroom discourse in the secondary school, across a number of different subjects; and the work of Pam Gilbert of James Cook University, Townsville, in Queensland, whose interests are both in writing in the secondary school, and in language and gender.

The signs are that a coherent educational linguistics is beginning to appear around the world, and I note with pleasure the appearance of two new and valuable international journals: *Language and Education*, edited by David Corson of Massey University, New Zealand, and *Linguistics in Education*, edited by David Bloome, of the University of Massachusetts. Both are committed to the development of an educational linguistics, to which many traditions of study, linguistic, semiotic and sociological, will no doubt make an important contribution. Such an educational linguistics is long overdue, and in what are politically difficult times, I suggest such a study can make a major contribution to the pursuit of educational equality of opportunity, and to attacking the wider social problems of equity and justice. Language is a political institution: those who are wise in its ways, capable of using it to shape and serve important personal and social goals, will be the ones who are 'empowered' (to use a fashionable word): able, that is, not merely to participate effectively *in* the world, but able also *to act upon it*, in the sense that they can strive for significant social change. Looked at in these terms, provision of appropriate language education programs is a profoundly important matter, both in ensuring equality of educational opportunity, and in helping to develop those who are able and willing to take an effective role in democratic processes of all kinds.

One of the most encouraging measures of the potential value of the perspectives open to teachers taking up an educational linguistics of the kind offered in these monographs, has been the variety of teachers attracted to the courses of which they form a part, and the ways in which these teachers have used what they have learned in undertaking research papers for the award of the master's degree. They include, for example, secondary teachers of physics, social science, geography and English, specialists in teaching English as a second language to migrants and specialists in teaching English to Aboriginal people, primary school teachers, a nurse educator, teachers of illiterate adults, and language curriculum consultants, as well as a number of teacher educators with specialist responsibilities in teaching language education. For many of these people the perspectives offered by an educational linguistics are both new and challenging, causing them to review and change aspects of their teaching practices in various ways. Coming to terms with a semantically driven grammar is in itself quite demanding, while there is often considerable effort involved to bring to conscious awareness the ways in which we use language for the realisation of different meanings. But the effort is plainly worth it, principally because of the added sense of control and direction it can give teachers interested to work at fostering and developing students who are independent and confident in using language for the achievement of various goals. Those people for whom these books have proved helpful, tend to say that they have achieved a stronger and richer appreciation of language and how it works than they had before; that because they know considerably more about language themselves, they are able to intervene much more effectively in directing and guiding those whom they teach; that because they have a better sense of the relationship of language and 'content' than they had before, they can better guide their students into control of the 'content' of the various subjects for which they are responsible; and finally, that because they have an improved sense of how to direct language learning, they are able to institute new assessment policies, negotiating, defining and clarifying realistic goals for their students. By any standards, these are considerable achievements.

As I draw this Foreword to a close, I should perhaps note for the reader's benefit the manner in which students doing course work with me are asked to read the monographs in this series, though I should stress that the books were deliberately designed to be picked up and read in any order one likes. In the first of the two semester courses, called *Language and Learning*, students are asked to read the following volumes in the order given:

Frances Christie — *Language education*
Clare Painter — *Learning the mother tongue*
M.A.K. Halliday & Ruqaiya Hasan — *Language, context, and
    text: aspects of language in a social-semiotic perspective*
J.L. Lemke — *Using language in the classroom*
then either,
M.A.K. Halliday — *Spoken and written language*
or,
Ruqaiya Hasan — *Linguistics, language, and verbal art.*

The following four volumes, together with the one by Michael Christie, mentioned above, belong to the second course called *Sociocultural Aspects of Language and Education*, and they may be read by the students in any order they like, though only three of the five need be selected for close study:

David Butt — *Talking and thinking: the patterns of
    behaviour*
Gunther Kress — *Linguistic processes in sociocultural practice*
J.R. Martin — *Factual writing: exploring and challenging
    social reality*
Cate Poynton — *Language and gender: making the difference*

References

Bain, A., *An English Grammar* (Longman, Roberts and Green, London, 1863).

Bain, A., *English Composition and Rhetoric*, revised in two Parts — *Part 1, Intellectual Elements of Style*, and *Part 11, Emotional Qualities of Style* (Longman, Green and Company, London, 1887).

Ballard, P., *Teaching the Mother Tongue* (Hodder & Stoughton, London, 1921).

Blair, H., *Lectures on Rhetoric and Belles Lettres, Vols. 1 and 11* (W. Strahan and T. Cadell, London, 1783).

Campbell, G., (new ed.), *The Philosophy of Rhetoric* (T. Tegg and Son, London, 1838). Originally published (1776).

Halliday, M.A.K., *Language as social semiotic: the social interpretation of language and meaning* (Edward Arnold, London, 1978).

Halliday, M.A.K., *An Introduction to Functional Grammar* (Edward Arnold, London, 1985).

Murray, Lindley, *English Grammar* (1795), Facsimile Reprint No. 106 (Menston, Scolar Press, 1968).

Contents

Introduction

This book represents a conversation. In the first place, it is a conversation between a student of educational theory and a student of linguistics. Moreover, it is a discussion about issues which the students have confronted during the study and practice of their different disciplines. As it happens, the participants have known each other right throughout their own educations. Still, while the talk is part of many past (and future) discussions, the dialogue is organised in order to be accessible and coherent to an outsider. In fact, the text is primarily directed to post-graduates who are working as external students.

The source of coherence is a theme: namely, the relation between talking and thinking. This theme is, of course, an ancient topic of human discourse. As a result of a process of evolution many of the forms of this discourse have become so specialised as to appear arcane. On the other hand, the discussion of language and thought is renewed with the reflections of even the kindergarten child in our community.

(Ch = girl, five years two months; Ad = adult/father)

Ad How did you know the answer was 'purple'?
Ch I was saying it in my mind.
Ad What do you mean you were saying it in your mind?
Ch I was meaning it in my mind.
Ad You were meaning it . . .?
Ch I know it in my mind.
(Moving on to a problem requiring the answer 'orange')
Ad Did you know 'orange' in your mind too?
Ch Yes, because 'orange' starts with /o/ and 'Oliver' and 'Otto' . . .

The present text elaborates a particular interpretation of what it means to talk and think. The interpretation itself differs from others in the literature in that it begins with a close examination of a theory of signs. The theory of sign then constitutes the bench-mark from which the discourse on talking and thinking goes forward: all discussion looks back to the strictures and implications of that theory.

The argument of this book might be summarised in the following way: the mental life of the individual is an artefact of the sign systems of the community. This formulation stresses the derivative status of subjective experience—the patterns of our thinking and feeling are given by the forms of our public talk: our objective signs are prior to what appear to be our private thoughts.

The argument goes forward in three general moves. In the first discussion, the Saussurean theory of the sign is closely examined, and that theory is seen in the context of alternative approaches to meaning. In the second discussion, the implications of sign theory are illustrated with respect to the description of thinking in particular communities. The discussion in this section also reviews controversies concerning universals, perception, and the status of a meta-language (that is, a language for describing a language). The third discussion extends the debate of the earlier sections by stressing the function of 'point of view' in the meaning potential of the community. By analysing different forms of discourse—the talk of five-year-olds; modern poetry—the 'intellect' is related to the community resources for taking point of view as the very subject-matter of discourse. The discussion ends by reflecting on a 'philosophy of as if'.

There are a number of reasons for the dialogue form of this book. The primary practical consideration was that it might be, in a small way, a surrogate for the tutorial discussion which the external student often has to forego. In other respects the dialogue is a formal echo of the themes in this text, namely, that we construct our knowledge through talk; and therefore, that our thinking is the present state of our conversations. Furthermore, it seemed probable that the accessibility of the material would be enhanced if the text were organised around more than just the point of view of a linguist.

Discussion

The role of thought in a theory of signs

David   Because language is realised or manifested in sounds, and at another level in words and grammar, it seems likely to me that many people find it easier to accept the idea of talking as a form of behaviour than to accept the notion that thinking is a form of behaviour.

Paull   Well, do you mean by behaviour here, merely something that an individual does? Or are you using behaviour to refer only to what people do that is common, shared, or normative across a group or culture?

David   Yes. This point is important. The force of the word behaviour for me involves the idea of public-ness. At least, I would emphasise this aspect more than is typical in the usage of the layman or in academic circles. I am claiming that we get our thinking from other people—or better that we construct it with others.

Paull   I can see, then, the point of the stress you are placing on language.

David   One point is that the others with whom we are constructing are not merely our contemporaries. The language of a culture is an evolved—evolving system. It is, in a sense, the activities of preceding generations working on us, with us, and within us. It creates a semantic atmosphere of a constant and consistent pressure which we adapt to perhaps much like our bodies and bones have become adapted to the atmosphere and gravity of living on earth.

Paull   You do say that whatever activities one undertakes as a thinker, these are built on a kind of bedrock of human experience as a speaker . . .

David   Yes . . .

Paull   But I take it that you are **not** saying that all thinking is in natural language. Is that right?

David   Hmm. That's a good point for me to take up here. What I have to do may look like something of a retreat. . .But we need

3

to introduce the idea of a sign system—an idea somewhat broader than that of a natural language. The meanings of a culture—what were referred to above through the metaphor of a semantic atmosphere—clearly extend beyond the linguistic system as it is conventionally described by linguists: namely, in terms of a semantics, a lexico-grammar, and a phonology. There is a problem here: those traditions of linguistics which emphasise social context as another level of description—for example, the British School after Firth and Malinowski—have also been the traditions which emphasise meanings in linguistic description. With Halliday's concept of 'meaning potential' the aim of description is to make explicit the resources for meaning which the member of the society has. As I suggested above, these resources extend beyond the narrow definition of language. If one is tempted, as I have been at different times, to broaden the terms 'language' and 'grammar', two kinds of difficulties arise. First of all, your methods of analysis can become ad hoc, since you are probably running together phenomena which need to be handled on quite distinct levels of description. And secondly, as Halliday himself points out, if you want to redefine grammar, or any other term, that is alright; but be prepared then to create a new term for what everyone else calls grammar.

To summarise the situation as I see it then: our conventional notion of language is too narrow to encompass all the possibilities of meaning across a culture. Yet I am rather wary of drawing a distinct boundary between language and other systems of signs. At the very least all systems of meaning in a culture interpenetrate, and in varying degrees. Hence I see, for example, our systems of mathematical meaning as very much part of the linguistic system, even though their ability to cross some linguistic boundaries suggests that they are special in a certain way. On the other hand with respect to art, music, and other more pragmatic systems (which are often described metaphonically as language, e.g. the 'languages of art'), I am not sure how they are best treated in a description.

But certainly, to return to your question—the public, social, linguistic basis of thinking as I view it, does not imply that all thinking has to be in a natural language, but rather thinking is constructed out of all the meaning systems assimilated from the context of culture. Here again a Hallidayan term is helpful: SOCIAL SEMIOTIC. Semiotic refers to sign systems. The social semiotic is what the individual assimilates. Of this, language is a rather tightly organised core—the semiotic system *par excellence*, to quote Saussure.

M. A. K. Halliday, *Language as Social Semiotic*, Edward Arnold, London, 1978

Paull   Okay then, let me go over that in my own terms. According to your view, thinking may not be in words; but the things that psychologists refer to when they're analysing thinking are the consequence of language . . .?

David   . . . The consequence of a sign system, a semiotic system. . .

4

Paull   Right . . . the consequence of participation in the
community systems of meaning.

David   Yes. That is a good formulation.

David   It is, I feel, the linguist's uncommon angle on semiosis—
the process of making signs—which leads him or her to view
thinking in terms of meaning systems. This is the point which,
for my part, I would like to see elaborated even before we
discuss the remarkable empirical studies relevant to this
conversation.

Paull   Fine. Only your use of the word linguist suggests there is
considerable consensus on a matter which is generally not even
regarded as linguistic. At other times you have made me aware
of the significant differences between linguistic theories. What's
going on?

David   Again, you're right to pull me up there. In fact, the
orientation to thinking from which I will argue is not at all
accepted across the whole community of linguists. The linguists
greatly influenced by Chomsky, for example, have a theory
which is the very antithesis of a social semiotic approach. As has
been noted the Chomskyan perspective is essentially an intra-
organism theory: it is innatist—Chomsky views the human
faculty for language as evidence of a species-specific mental
organ; and the theory is also committed to the idea of an abstract
grammar which is latent in all natural languages and which, in
being universal, reflects certain deep principles in the
organisation of **the** human mind. Chomsky himself is explicit
about seeing linguistics as a 'branch of psychology'.

Furthermore his work has been linked (again by Chomsky
himself) with the tradition of philosophy deriving from Déscartes.
Cartesian philosophy is especially noted for its 'dualism'—its
sharp distinction between mind and non-mind.

Paull   So there is an intra-organism linguistics, is there? An
approach to language which does not begin in society and
behaviour.

David   Oh, there certainly is. My own views, however, derive as I
have said, from linguistic traditions in which linguistics is always,
in a sense, socio-linguistics. But I see this schism in linguistics as
essentially a result of how different linguists have assimilated the
insights of Ferdinand de Saussure—the Swiss linguist whose
concepts have made contemporary linguistics possible. These
concepts have also provided the basis for structuralist theories
across a number of disciplines.

What I will argue is that it is through the ideas of Saussure
that the linguist has a special angle for talking about thinking and
the mind. While Chomsky has always argued that the linguist
does have this special angle—almost a privileged access—
Chomsky's approach derives nothing of its methodology from
Saussure, with the possible exception of one point which I regard
as a misreading of the Saussurean concepts.

**Linguistics and
the study of the
mind**

Noam Chomsky,
*Reflections on
Language*, Pantheon
Books, New York,
1975, p.36

Ferdinand de
Saussure, *Course in
General Linguistics*,
ed. C. Bally & A.
Sechehaye in
collaboration with
A. Riedlinger,
Fontana/Collins,
Glasgow, 1978

5

Paull So, to understand the basis of your descriptions of thinking and consciousness, I am going to need to understand Saussure. Is that right?

David Yes. To a degree. And in order to understand how views on the mind can be so divergent, even in a single discipline like linguistics, we should also note how Saussure's ideas have been differently employed in linguistics.

Paull So the Saussurean theory is going to provide some kind of framework for me in discussing the more empirical and observational material I know we are going to consider. . .?

David Yes. I thought, originally, that it would be advisable to begin with actual ethnographic and cross-cultural studies. Since then, I have changed—I feel the Saussurean concepts and certain other abstract points are best offered at the outset. Then they can be turned over and over as we attempt the exemplification of issues. It is worth noting also, that Saussure's ideas relate mainly to clarifying the relationship between thought and sound-images in a linguistic system. By beginning with Saussure, we are beginning at the very interface between thought and sound within the linguistic sign.

Paull Fine. I'm ready to hear about the 'Saussurean legacy', particularly as, if I understand you correctly, it is going to be crucial to my own analytical methods. You are suggesting, aren't you, that the linguist has a highly developed way of analysing language; and that this methodology is helpful when applied to other aspects of behaviour?

Analysing behaviour: atomism versus structuralism

David Well, let's see. What if we begin by considering the general problem of analysing behaviour? The whole idea of analysis implies proceeding from a complex structure to elements or units or constituents; or perhaps, more accurately, to a configuration of the elements. The guiding metaphor here is that of 'atomism': namely, that some things are complex and some simple. It has probably been almost the syndrome of scientists that their job involves breaking up some entity until it reveals its basic units of composition.

Paull You're drawing attention here, of course, to much that goes on outside science as well.

Bertrand Russell, *An Inquiry into Meaning and Truth*, Penguin Books, Harmondsworth, 1973, p.28. See also J. Watling on Russell on an Ideal Language in John Watling, *Bertrand Russell*, Oliver and Boyd, Edinburgh, 1970.

David Yes. Atomism is, in fact, part of Western ideology. It is now part of the everyday assumptions of which we are hardly aware. In academic circles, however, I think atomism may have passed its heyday. The remarkable history of physics in the first decades of this century seemed to give the metaphor its dynamism.

Paull So, the metaphor turns up in diverse places: in the philosophy of Bertrand Russell, for example, in 'logical atomism'.

David Yes. Russell's logical atomism is essentially a theory about language, or at least about propositions and the world. So too, the early philosophy of Wittgenstein with its pursuit of 'simples'. The same principle is operating in such theories: namely, that something complex is built out of the combination of simpler 'constituents'. Behaviourism in American psychology is another case in point.

Paull   Certainly, since the behaviourist program was to describe all complex behaviour in terms of the 'atom' of conditioning: stimulus-response and reinforcement.

David   Now many of these programs—Russell's in philsophy, and Watson, Skinner et al., in psychology—need to be seen in the context of an attempt to break away from what they regarded as non-empirical hocus-pocus. They were, in a sense, attempts to give a materialist account of aspects of reality. What such programs overlooked, however, was **not** overlooked by another materialist thinker—the Russian psychologist Vygotsky.

On the psychology of Watson and Skinner, see Chapter 1 and 2 in Arthur Koestler, *The Ghost in the Machine*, Pan Books, London, 1970.

   Vygotsky stressed that in the analysis of a complex phenomenon one must be careful that the basic units are not out of character with the very factor which you are pursuing. Hence, he notes, it is of little use to expend all your energies examining the isolated gases hydrogen and oxygen if your aim is to understand the properties of water, even though we are all aware that these gases are elemental with respect to the compound H_2O.

L. S. Vygotsky, *Thought and Language*, MIT Press, Massachusetts, 1962

Paull   What I see this as meaning, for the study of behaviour, is that high order activities may not be simply explicable in terms of lower order constituents.

David   I agree with that interpretation. The higher order becomes a new system, not merely an aggregate of elements. In the teaching sphere, Vygotsky notes that when a child has learnt a certain set of basic mathematical operations—addition, subtraction, division, multiplication—he or she has developed a body of related procedures. However, when that same child adds an understanding of algebra to this repertoire, the whole structure of his mathematical understanding is transformed—the earlier operations are still 'there', but they have a different place, function, or value in the system of the child's understanding. There is, in fact, a new system which has evolved out of the preceding system.

an example in the teaching sphere of the psychology of Vygotsky

Paull   And, of course, the child cannot go back and retrieve the old way of looking at numbers.

David   No, the child cannot go back. We can be rusty about something we've learnt, but in conceptual shifts like the one I just described we cannot become blind, so to speak, to the relationships that we've learnt to see.

Paull   I think I can see your drift and your destination more clearly now. It's clearer to me at least why you might say that we learn to think or at least we learn particular ways of thinking.

David   To illustrate what you've just said, it is appropriate at this stage to prefigure the empirical studies to be discussed at our next meeting.

Vygotsky and his team of psychologists, which included the psychologist/neuro-physiologist Alexander Luria, studied various Uzbek and Kirghiz communities in Central Asian Russia during the communisation period of 1930–32. These cotton growing and pastoralist communities were virtually lifted from feudalism into machine agriculture, rudimentary education, corporate decision-making. . .Now the psychologists, actually witnessed changes in patterns of thinking, changes that were more fundamental than the small example above concerning algebra. In fact, the changes were in many cases related to reasoning and classifying which we, in our cultural context, might call 'a priori'—as if they existed prior to any information from experience, as if they didn't have to be learnt because they were inherent in reality! But that must wait.

Paull   Well, you were just explaining the limitations of atomism, at least as it applies to studies of behaviour.

David   Its limitations have become evident across many disciplines. In physics, for instance, the progress seemed to falter: on the one hand the kind of total description which the empiricist program envisaged was ruled out, not just for practical reasons, but in theory also. On the other hand, the pursuit of a 'basic' particle has become more ambiguous—with a proliferation of subatomic particles.

Paull   If the success of the atomism metaphor has waned, what notions replaced it?

David   I would say 'function'; and along with function also 'structure' or 'pattern'. But these three terms have to be considered in the context of a 'system', or what is often now called a 'model'. And all of these notions bring us to Saussure.

Paull   Very well. But perhaps a small illustration would help me assess the general point you are making concerning 'units' of behaviour. How do you react to, say, the common distribution observed in psychology, and education, between aspects of a task related to 'cognition' and aspects described as 'affect'?

David   The distinction is a good instance to review in that it is also made by numerous theorists in semantics. It seems to me an example of the kind of practical heuristic step often adopted in the analysis of human behaviour—that is, the analysis proceeds 'as if' there were two such autonomous factors operating in reality. At first, the distinction appears to be a liberation. In semantic theory it seemed, for example, that a great rigour could be introduced into the description of word and sentence meanings because one could focus on a kind of core meaning which, it was said, always operated with the item in question. It was suggested that around this core, or nucleus (note the imagery of atoms), there is a cluster of more indeterminate factors which are, so the story goes, too variable to be brought into a formal semantic theory. Of course, cognitive meaning became the kind of 'real' meaning and the theorists had established a legitimacy, at least in their view, for proceeding with language models which virtually omitted the social-pragmatic and contextual dimensions of speech.

It seems to me that the kind of analysis I have just outlined is contrary to Saussurean theory. Rather it owes its orientation to the formalist tradition of language philosophy—Frege and Russell. In this tradition language is examined in terms of producing true, unequivocal propositions about an objectified external world. The unit of language typically in focus is something like a short isolated sentence—something amenable to reformulation in a logical language. There is nothing approaching the linguist's notion of text. Furthermore, such a tradition seems, to an outsider like myself, to have been fixated by the idea that meaning is to be understood in terms of the conditions under which a proposition would be true or false.

Paull Ah. That of course is taking us back to the logical positivists earlier in this century: they were, perhaps, the group most determined to see the whole world and all meaning according to the canons of empirical science.

David Now there is a crucial feature common to the semanticists with their 'cognitive meanings', Russell and his referential theory of language, and the logical positivists with their idea of meaning.

In all these views, it seems to me, the nature of reality is taken as given. Reality is not constructed by community members in a three-way interaction between themselves, others, and a wider context of conditions and actions. Reality is in some sense 'there'; and it is the task of language and the mind to make reliable correspondences between external events, channels of perceptual information, and internal brain states.

Paull This latter view would be, I think, a fair description of what Western communities broadly accept.

David Maybe. But this general view has been disestablished across many disciplines. 'Correspondence' is just too simple. And this is now apparent, even in the subjects which first seemed to confirm the correspondence view. In physics, the crucial change related to the observer, to the fact that, ultimately, observers are participants in the micro- and macro- events of the universe. In philosophy, there was a shift in the understanding of thinking and language—a change mainly associated with the later work of Wittgenstein. His investigations show that the recognition of 'private' experiences (emotions, pains etc.) depends on our having assimilated the 'public' criteria of a language. But these matters we can elaborate after we consider Saussure.

Paull Certainly, in my recent readings in psycho-analysis and counselling, one is often struck by how much seems to be lost in the analytical procedure. To return to my example of cognition versus affect: it's not just that one loses out by putting aside the global perspective, it's that one of the elements is typically accorded primacy over the other.

Look also, for instance, at the degree of attention accorded cognitive tasks in schooling. There is an explicit syllabus and everyone's eyes are on exam results. If parents enquire about the more immediate character of the school as a socialising institution, it is often a concern about 'discipline'.

David On that last observation concerning what gets primacy, it has interested me in my own observations of a child starting school that so many aspects of the school are working simultaneously on the child's experience. For example, from the parent and teacher perspective, the fundamental revolution going on for the child is learning to read and write. This cognitive development is changing the whole structure of the child's sense of the world and its possibilities. From the perspective of my five-year-old daughter, however, the society of the classroom and playground is all bound up in the experience of learning: she appears to note carefully the actions and proclivities of all the school children with whom she comes in contact. And her observations are the subject of precise reports, even more than the words and sentences learnt. The sexual politics of talking and playing with boys is also very prominent. And I daresay these aspects of kindergarten—the social pragmatic aspects—are central to **her** experience and enthusiasm.

But on the more abstract point concerning primacy, I don't think there is any accident over what element of a theory is or is not given primacy. Rather, the reasons are a reflection of the ideology of the tradition within which the analysis is conducted. This was the point of my observations on formal semantics and its precursors. The cognitivist bias could not have emerged from a strictly Saussurean tradition.

Paull Okay. Explain what it is about Saussurean theory that is relevant to what we have discussed so far about complex behaviour, and its analysis into elements or units.

The Saussurean concepts: from dichotomy to paradox

David Saussure's legacy is a set of concepts from which the analysis of human language can proceed without the analysis putting at risk the essential character of language as a system. Overall, this legacy of concepts involves a shift away from the notion of constituent entities or items, and toward the idea that a semiotic system is totally based on relationships. In order to understand this reorientation to what can be called 'structuralist analysis', we ought to consider a sequence of dichotomies which are explained in the *Course in General Linguistics*: a book compiled by Saussure's students and published after his death in 1913.

Paull What was Saussure himself trained in? Not linguistics as we regard it today, I suppose?

David No. He was trained in the grammatical and philological studies of the second half of the nineteenth century. That is, he was trained to view languages historically and comparatively; as he put it: 'diachronically', or through time. But what he sought in the most important part of his *Course* was to clarify the methodology of a 'SYNCHRONIC' LINGUISTICS—a linguistics of the system that speakers hold in common.

Paull   So the diachronic/synchronic distinction is the first step in the method? As such, it is the first step in a process of idealisation, isn't it?

David   Yes to both questions. As we've discussed it, analysis will always involve some form of idealisation. And furthermore, the fact that language is never totally static, never completely synchronic, has been one of the chief points of criticism of Saussure's approach.

The next dichotomy relates to the terms *langue* and *parole*. Saussure distinguishes between language (*langue*)—which is what the individuals have in common across a community; and speaking (*parole*)—the 'sum of particular acts' of speech produced by the individuals in the community. It is helpful to regard this distinction as the difference between looking at language as a collective phenomenon and looking at it in terms of the actual products of individuals. Saussure stresses that linguistics is concerned with the shared system, not with the total of the individual output. I should add Saussure saw these, *langue* and *parole*, as interdependent: language is 'both the instrument and product' of speaking. But in Saussurean analysis one has to come to terms with elements which depend on one another yet are 'absolutely distinct'.

Saussure, p. 9

Paull   This is the kind of point relevant to your view that these dichotomies are paradoxical, or in some sense, counter-intuitive?

David   From this point on that becomes increasingly so. The paradoxes begin, I suppose, when Saussure stresses, at the outset of the *Course* that 'it is the viewpoint that creates the object' of study in linguistics. That is to say, the phenomena are not just there to be described; they are not just given. Saussure wrongly thought that this situation was special to the science of linguistics. In fact, as our earlier comments concerning the observer in physics might have suggested, the idea that the point of view or the theory creates the 'object' is now a commonplace of scientific understanding. It is one of the quintessential features of intellectual modernity. Saussure arrived at this methodological insight before it became widely recognised. For example, it is now forcefully urged by the philosopher Nelson Goodman, in his *Ways of World Making*, that there is no reason to assume that different descriptions of reality might all be reduced to one reality, **the** reality; particularly as the methods of reduction would be themselves so various.

Saussure, p. 8

But the paradoxical side of the Saussurean method emerges as we come to focus on his concept of a sign. At first there appears to be no difficulty: a linguistic sign is a two-part structure.

Figure 1

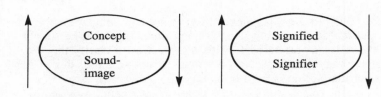

Saussure, pp. 66, 114

Paull   Well. How does this two-part structure differ from say the referential theories you have previously rejected—for example, with respect to Russell?

David   In many crucial ways. First of all, in referential and naming theories only the sound image, the signifier, is the sign. In Saussure, pp. 65–7 Saussure's theory the two parts of the sign cannot be separated. In referential theories, the relationship is actually between a concrete thing or state of affairs and a sound. In Saussure's Saussure, pp. 65–7 theory the 'linguistic sign . . . is a two-sided psychological entity'—it is the combination of a concept and an acoustic image. To understand the psychological status of the acoustic image (*signifiant*) just keep your lips and tongue still and then put together in your mind a group of rhyming words. Then ask yourself how you knew they rhymed; because you could compare the 'psychological imprint' of the sounds.

The most important differences are yet to be explained. They relate to the origin and place of a sign in its system.

In referential and naming theories the entity referred to or named is given; it's already a unit before the reference or naming takes place. In Saussurean theory, neither the phonic substance in Saussure, p. 112 which language is realised nor the realm of thought 'yield pre-delimited entities'. What Saussure suggests here is paradoxical Saussure, p. 112 for most readers. Saussure himself calls it a 'mysterious fact': namely, that language can be pictured 'as a series of contiguous subdivisions marked off on both the indefinite plane of jumbled ideas (A) and the equally vague plane of sounds (B)'.

Figure 2

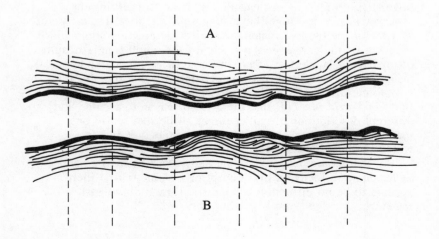

Saussure goes on to say that 'the characteristic role of language with respect to thought is not to create a material phonic means for expressing ideas but to serve as a link between thought and sound, under conditions that of necessity bring about the reciprocal delimitations of units'.

Saussure, p. 112

Paull   Yes. This is certainly a contrast to all correspondence theories of language and thought since, here, the two parts of the sign are mutually defining.

David   I think that's what Saussure means when he claims that 'language works out its units' while taking shape between two shapeless masses (thought and sound).

The reciprocal delimitation has a paradoxical character since, in Saussure's words: 'Thought, chaotic by nature, has to become ordered in the process of its decomposition'. It is the delimitation of thought with sound that produces the 'form'; and Saussure stresses that language is form not 'substance'.

Saussure, p. 112

Paull   Is there some other example of the same process which might help to clarify this delimitation?

David   It seems to me that this kind of delimitation lies at the heart of all complex systems. But jumping from one discipline to another may not help at this point in the explanation. One merely tries to envisage the way a system might 'work out its own units'.

Saussure, p. 112

Paull   Your comments about the *signifié* in relation to the *signifiant* really must apply beyond each individual sign; at least, I take the diagram (A ←—→ B) to represent a number of signs alongside one another.

David   In fact, the paradox deepens as we widen our focus to take on the fuller implications of that diagram. You're right to make me explain this horizontal relationship between signs, for it brings us to a further cornerstone in Saussure's theory.

The first step is to distinguish between the concepts of signification and value. Saussure offers us a further diagram to clarify this distinction.

Figure 3

Saussure, p. 115

Now it would seem, given the description of the sign presented earlier, that the vertical relationship between *signifié* (signified) and *signifiant* (signifier) delimits both the conceptual and the phonic units. But this is not the full picture. In focusing on one sign, it is easy to overlook the fact that a signified is only what it is because of its contrast with the other signifieds. Expressed more dramatically, a signified is what it is because of what it is not—it is defined negatively with respect to all other

13

signifieds in the system. The same point needs to be made concerning the signifier. Hence, the two elements of a sign are delimited by the combination of both the vertical relations **and** the horizontal relations.

Therefore, a concept is delimited by two kinds of relation: (a) the concept's bond with a sound image (vertical arrows); and (b) that concept's place alongside other concepts with which it contrasts (the horizontal arrows).

This is not an easy point, by any means. But it is essential to understanding the importance of Saussure's insights.

Paull   I think I can identify why both kinds of relations are necessary. If you are describing a sign system then you cannot stop at the description of a single sign.

David   That is true; but there's more than that. Saussure points out that in analysis one cannot start with isolated terms, add them together, and thereby arrive at the system. The two kinds of relations, the vertical (signification) and the horizontal (value) are a means for capturing the interdependence of the whole system.

This is perhaps the point at which one sees the widest gulf between, say, referential theories and Saussure's theory of a semiotic system. When one understands the interdependence of signification and value, language is not treated as an aggregate of individual acts of reference or of naming. It was only after a long, arduous campaign that a related insight emerged in modern analytical philosophy. Again, it was Wittgenstein who argued that traditional accounts of language were in error since they assumed the existence of what they set out to explain. For example, language could not have developed through acts of naming because to make sense of the activity of naming one needs to be already familiar with language.

Paull   So signification and value, then, are essential concepts for linguistic, or semiotic, analysis because:

1   they permit one to address a totality of signs; and
2   they bring out the relationships, the interdependencies across the totality of signs.

David   If we just change the wording somewhat in your point (2), I think it, by itself, gets to the central issue. It is through signification and value that one can give appropriate emphasis to the character of language as a system—the systematicity of language. So it is through these concepts that Saussure sought to clarify the interdependencies within a semiotic system.

Paull   Now, what if we take this point back to Vygotsky's example: namely that you can't clarify the properties of water by studying hydrogen and oxygen as isolates. Perhaps we ought to look back to our general discussion of the analysis of behaviour.

David   Yes. The relevance is very direct. What we rejected about the atomism metaphor was the implication that analysis was a search for more and more basic 'items'. Certainly this is now a caricature of what any contemporary scientist could possibly believe he was doing. But it affects everyone in a teaching/academic community to some extent—it has become part of our cultural assumptions about what it is to know. It lies behind the enormous funding that maintains the pursuit of the quark in physics.

As we noted earlier, the metaphor which has grown out of, and superseded, atomism is the idea of the scientist creating models. Is there a subject area in science that does not build models? In particular, subjects like economics and linguistics have been very preoccupied with models, just as in physics earlier this century, one had competing models of the atom: the Rutherford model, the Bohr model.

Now, I think one can say that Saussure's concepts have been very important in establishing this era of the model. This is because Saussure brings his reader face to face with what holds a model together: namely, units based on relationships of contrast or opposition.

Paull   So, by contrast with the item approach, in Saussure we meet relations.

David   Yes; and I suspect **only** relations. The units do not have some essential core plus a penumbra of relations; the relations are the core, if you like, though I personally feel uneasy about cores, kernels, and such everyday metaphors of atomism.

Paull   However, I take it that an important aspect of the relations of contrast is that they must always entail a system, for one can only have oppositions in something which is more than an aggregate. Am I getting too abstract here? I wonder if we can, in fact, bring these paradoxes down to earth.

David   Well, it would be my claim that once we can envisage our social environments in terms of relational units, then the earth never looks the same again—structure leaps out at you, since you can see that behind certain kinds of variation there may well be a common principle of contrast, the kind of consistency one interprets as a pattern.

Applications

Paull   What about the issue of application in the educational sphere? Where do these concepts have a place?

David   In any domain which you identify as a system of conventions—with any system of meanings, in the first place.

Paull   Clearly then, the Saussurean notion of a system of relations is going to help in the understanding of language. But that seems rather indirect to me, at least in terms of the practical concerns of a teacher.

David   We're not through the concepts, yet. But before we continue, let's mention some areas in which the idea of relational units has been important.

Handbooks on structuralism often use the study of phonology as the best way into the importance of relations.

Phonology is the study of the sound systems of natural languages. The linguist Troubetzkoy is given credit for clarifying how the actual sounds made by the speakers of a language need to be distinguished from the set of sounds which make meaningful contrasts for these speakers. For example, in English the two phonemes /t/ and /d/ constitute a significant opposition. We can see this opposition working in what are called minimal pairs (the words 'tin' and 'din'). On the other hand, in most Australian Aboriginal languages there is no such significant opposition. A speaker of Pitjantjatjara can drift between the two similar sounds (phonetically [t] and [d]) and not put his communication at risk.

Paull Because no meaning depends on hearing the difference. . .?

David Yes. And of course, it is very hard to hear a contrast that does not have a 'function' in one's own system. The phonetic 'reality', so as to speak, is difficult to discern if it does not have a function in one's phonological system.

Paull I can see also, from this example, why one can talk about the 'social construction of reality'.

David How do you mean?

Paull Well, the reality of the /t/ and /d/ distinction exists for the English speaker; but it has no existence for the speaker of Pitjantjatjara. In this small way different realities have been constructed through the collective practices of the group.

David Yes. The situation is indicative of the way systems vary. If they vary, it follows that such systems are not made up of givens—they are not natural but conventional.

Paull And if they are conventional, they are an artefact of the culture: so the 'construction' metaphor is apt.

David The difficulty one has with the actual perception of contrasts from another system is very interesting too, don't you think? The situation shows that perception is not a neutral channel to one external reality.

Paull Yes. I agree. If another system is difficult to perceive, then it is clear that habitual activities—one's experiences, in other words—affect perception.

David This point will be very important when we review the information gathered by Vygotsky and Luria—the studies from Uzbekistan and Kirghizia during communisation. Speech research has actually given this point concerning perception a double edge. On the one hand, there is the cross-cultural or cross-system phenomenon of perceiving contrasts which are not significant in one's own system. On the other hand, there is also something of a mystery as to how we are able to extract as much information as we do from the acoustic messages that speakers actually exchange.

One theory put forward suggests that our motor experience as speakers/articulators permits us to decode beyond the quality of acoustic signal.

Paull I imagine the context of a message has a good deal to do with its comprehension, also.

David Yes. The motor theory of speech perception does bring out, as well, the degree to which perception depends on collective experience.

Still, we should get back to the applications of a theory of relations.

Paull Economics would be a field outside linguistics, would it not? One branch of economics is concerned with the construction of models; and it strikes me that in an economic system the values and significations are constantly changing and being reinterpreted.

David I'm sure both the model building as well as the political-historical branches of economics are clarified when the subject is viewed as a system of relations. Although I am not clear on how the terms signification and value themselves would undergo a change when taken out of the study of communication.

If we move to literary analysis, it is clear how the structuralist notion of relations of relations of relations etc. . .is needed to deal with the many levels of meaningful patterning that the writer constructs. The resources for contrasts or oppositions in a work of verbal art can be so skilfully organised by a writer that the theme of a work is actually articulated by the way the meanings of the text create patterns of consistency, or a semantic drift.

This topic is fully elaborated in Ruqaiya Hasan's volume, *Linguistics, Language, and Verbal Art*, Oxford University Press, Oxford, 1989.

Paull What about biology and the life sciences? It is often said that biological processes are exchanges of information. How is the relational approach relevant here, if at all.

David Well, let me offer one of a number of possible points here. The point relates to evolutionary theory. For an organism to be viable, its structure must meet two kinds of conditions—as Bateson has expressed them, there is the organism's 'internal demands for coherence' as well as 'external requirements of the environment'. The difficulties of envisaging the dual conditions operating systematically has, I think, much in common with the difficulties of 'reciprocal delimitation', and the concepts value and signification in Saussure's theory. Whatever the case, it is clear that the life sciences do not deal with items, but with increasingly complex systems of order. In these 'open' systems, much as in the case of language, the important concept is relational: what function x has with respect to the state of the system.

See the discussion of 'Binocular Vision' in Gregory Bateson, *Mind and Nature: A Necessary Unity*, Fontana/Collins, Glasgow, 1980, pp. 79–80.

Paull It strikes me, from what you have said so far concerning Saussure and systems, that we could put together a list of educational contexts in which the concepts apply. That is, we could consider these contexts more in relational terms.

David Okay. But two things we need to keep in mind are:

1 we haven't yet completed our review of Saussurean concepts;

2 analyses take a great deal of worrying through.

Let's agree to offer some suggestions now and, then, to come back to the issues in the light of a wider range of concepts and the empirical studies of the next discussion.

Paull Something that immediately comes to mind is how one would describe the processes of education. I say processes, because we've got so many perspectives to begin with: the teacher's; that of the students; the expectations of the parents; the place of education in the community.

David Well a general point that may be interesting relates to linearity. Like talking itself, the activities of educational institutions, even the activities of the teacher, unfold across time. They have to be made compatible with units of linearity. By contrast, knowledge and understanding, whether of the teacher or the student, have a non-linear character. This point emerges when one thinks back to the example of the child learning algebra. The child comes to control a new system.

Paull The Marxist concept of dialectic could be useful here, as it builds in both notions of linearity and a new synthesis.

David Perhaps. But there are many issues which need to be pondered.

Related to linearity, for example, is the concept of a SYNTAGM: a configuration of successive units. Now looking at lessons as syntagms may be helpful; especially as the notion of a syntagm depends on the kinds of choices that could actually function as the units in the syntagm. But syntagmatic and paradigmatic relations are one more of the Saussurean paradoxes—and we should concentrate on those in a moment.

J. L. Lemke, *Using Language in the Classroom*, Oxford University Press, Oxford, 1989.

Paull What about considering some of the central teaching situations? Does a teacher and a class constitute a system? How would the system perspective change the general habits of regarding a teacher and class?

David Yes, you've pulled me up sharply here. I wish we could settle the interactive units and the structure of classroom and school. Jay Lemke's volume should be reconsidered at this point. But so should Clare Painter's volume on language development and Halliday's *Learning How to Mean*. For if we think of learning situations more broadly, it's clear that the mother-child dyad is a kind of interactive unit. Some advantages of seeing the dyad as a system can be stated.

Clare Painter, *Learning the Mother Tongue*, Oxford University Press, Oxford, 1989.

Paull DYAD implies system, complementarity, relationship for me. The word has a special relevance in the school counselling of which I am now a part. It's certainly not just an item of jargon, meaning two people.

M. A. K. Halliday, *Learning How to Mean: Explorations in the Development of Language*, Edward Arnold, London, 1975

David No. . .I agree. In the mother-child context, 'system' means that the two participants are creating a 'potential' which neither could even begin to create in isolation. So their dyad is **not** the sum of the resources of two people.

Also important is the fact that between the mother and child the meaning potential appears to exhibit both continuity and change. Elements that have been realising meanings in the child's earliest systems of symbolic behaviour, may seem to be present in later stages of the child's development. I am referring to the period, say, between ten/eleven months and sixteen months. Such apparent continuities have to be interpreted, however, in the light of the evolving system of meanings between child and care-givers. What may appear to be a continuation must be seen against the new values and significations. As Saussure has emphasised, if an element has a different place *vis-à-vis* the system, then it is not the same element. This point concerning values is even more pressing in the study of early language development since between the proto-language stage and the period of transition (i.e. as the child is approaching the system of the mother tongue), the system of the dyad develops from a two-strata system to a three-strata structure. This evolution in the system gives the child the potential to map more than one function onto an expression. In fact it is the beginning of 'grammar' or 'form'—though not yet the grammar of the adult world.

Paull   What you are emphasising here, then, is that Saussurean concepts allow you to capture the order in the development. . .?

David   Yes. It seems to me that the mother-child dyad is a good illustration of a paradox: namely, that an evolving system of meanings or knowledge will always be, in some sense, built on what has gone before. But, in that the system takes on new relations of contrast and even new strata of relations, the evolved system is utterly different from what has gone before. One can see, I think, the importance of the concept of value in elucidating the structure of the dyad as a system of meanings. As I say, one should go over the studies by Halliday and Painter to examine this in detail.

Paull   An interesting point concerning Saussure's concept of value emerges from what you have said about dyad. Didn't you say previously that value was part of Saussure's approach to synchronic linguistics? Because, what seems clear about value is that it aids in comparing systems across time—diachronically—as well as synchronically.

David   I think that's true. And certain of Saussure's examples draw attention to this application across time.

Paull   I was also wondering whether schooling could be addressed as a system of synchronic systems; and whether the structure could be revealed and made coherent after the method of the development studies which you have mentioned.

David   Jay Lemke's approaches to the science classroom are part of this large undertaking. Also important is Ruquiya Hasan's project at Macquarie University. Hasan and Cloran have been analysing the style of interaction recorded in 24 mother-child

19

dyads. The dyads themselves are arranged into groups according to variables like the educational background of the mum etc. Certain children are now being recorded at home **and** school during their kindergarten year.

Paull   So the recordings span home and classroom activities?

David   Yes. And they permit the kind of close analysis which you mentioned above. The interactions recorded include: mother-child in various home settings when the child was three and a half years old: bathing, eating, dressing; peer group outside class; peer group in class; teacher-student in different lessons; and so on.

Paull   It seems to me that the Saussurean concepts are essentially tools for identifying consistencies, or structure, in a community.

David   Yes. They are, in my view, an important part of the general effort to describe the regularities of social experience. Such regularities are so much taken for granted that people come to accept their consequences as inexorable—as if in 'the nature of things'. For example, by not recognising the consistencies across systems within the overall system of the culture, we risk being instruments for the consolidation of inequalities. We will eventually give some time to discussing Bernstein's theory of language codes—a topic, I know you, Paull, have read carefully. Perhaps a few words at this point would help bring the Saussurean concepts into another domain relevant to education. The issue of codes also illustrates our point concerning the patterns in daily affairs.

Paull   The idea of codes, I agree, could have very great consequences for education—that is, if the whole matter could be clarified. In fact the topic is important when looked at from either of two perspectives: either from the point of view of what goes on in a school and classroom, as well as from the angle of understanding the society in which codes might evolve. But as I say, this importance all depends on the idea becoming less equivocal, less slippery. It has to be taken out of the discussion of language deficit, for example; otherwise it becomes like the IQ tests you mentioned earlier—a means of giving apparent substance to inequalities, a way of turning differences into a hierarchy.

David   I'm aware of the difficulties surrounding this topic and that's why I offer it as an area in which the relevance of Saussure's methodology can be seen.

   One of your earliest misgivings concerning codes was, as I recall, their status as a part of a science.

Paull   That's true. Following Popper's famous criterion of the SCIENTIFIC: namely, that a hypothesis was scientific to the degree that it was open to falsification, it struck me that 'codes' were an hypothesis that shifted ground. In short, it was a theory that could not state the conditions under which it might be falsified. This is, of course, a criticism quite distinct from saying 'codes do not exist'. I think my misgivings were well founded since it is plain from the controversy that surrounds the topic, the theory of codes is still equivocal for people working in educational fields.

David   My rejoinder here will address the equivocal nature of the theory as you have argued it. Tangentially I note that both of us would now be unhappy about Popper's definition of a science, given that, as shown by Lakatos and Feyerabend, it excludes so much of the actual history of 'science'. Still, back to codes.

My point is that the obstruction in the articulation and exploration of the theory has not been the responsibility of Bernstein, sociology, educational theory, etc. The obstruction has been in linguistics. The preoccupation of much linguistics during the 1960s and 1970s has been with formalising statements concerning syntax. What is crucial to the understanding of codes, however, is a pattern in meanings.

R. Hasan, 'Code, register and social dialect', in B. Bernstein (ed.), *Class, Codes and Control*, Routledge & Kegan Paul, London, 1971–1973–1975. See Extending the conversation.

Now the point is that the clarification of Bernstein's theory depended on the development of a grammar which could bring out semantic patterns—differences of orientation to meaning and acting. Language had to be seen as a form of doing. In Halliday's developments of systemic-functional theory, such a grammar is available. It is now feasible to search out contrasts and consistencies of semantic orientation in different contexts.

Halliday's grammar is Saussurean; in particular the sign in this model is always semantic and defined by relations—the meanings are a product of the delimitation of *signifiés* and *signifiants*. And the entire systemic-functional grammar is built around the notion of choice amongst a range of possible meanings, or values.

What went wrong with the reception of Bernstein's work was the tendency of the age to see codes in terms of the presence or absence of particular formal items. Rather than seek out the principles around which the meaning choices of different social groups are organised, there was a rush to test the theory according to the canons of formalism.

I argued earlier that, without Saussure's concepts, analysis was unable to capture the character of language as a system. So too with respect to codes—if one does not begin from a Saussurean point of view, characteristics of the object of study just never arise. In a sense, they do not exist unless the overall theory of language has a place for them. In a milieu of phrase structures, rules, and formalisation, it is not surprising that an aspect of language concerned with meanings, experience, and contexts should be misunderstood. Furthermore, amidst Chomskyan theories based on the 'competence' of the individual and on the idea of a genetic 'universal grammar', a theory based on the tendencies of groups and on semantic differences was out of step.

So one begins with Popper's criterion of falsification, but ends up with a situation more like Kuhn's idea of a clash of paradigms within the academic community.

Paull   Okay, I'll accept your view, in the main. I can see, for example, how the aims and methods of the Chomskyan era determined the object of study for many linguists, and other social scientists too. It is still not clear to me, however, how the Saussurean concepts are applied beneath the global level at which we have been talking.

David   Yes. There is nothing more convincing than seeing the oppositions and values emerging in your own analysis. But I have been holding out on you with respect to one of Saussure's most famous illustrations. And there are still four terms that need to be explained. Only when we have filled out these gaps would it be fair to say that we have considered the crucial role of thought **within** the very nature of a sign.

Thought and sign; thought and system

David   In my view, this fact cannot be overstressed: thought is implicated in a language system right from the very origins of that system. In other words a language is not a means for expressing thoughts, since this formulation implies that the form of the language and the thoughts are at some point separate. In the Saussurean approach, the significations and values create the possibilities of thought at the same time that they determine the signifiers. Recall: 'Thought, chaotic by nature, has to become ordered in the process of its decomposition'.

Saussure, p. 112

Given this Saussurean conception of sign, then, it also makes no sense to talk about purely formal aspects of linguistic structure. None of the structure of a language can be without involvement in thought or meaning. This point brings us back to the difficult concepts of the preceding paragraph. The difficulty relates to our desire to see language as the handmaid to thought, to separate out a form and a content. Having illegitimately separated them out, we then spend our lives seeking ways in which they can be reintegrated!

For instance, one of the perennial issues of linguistics, philosophy, and literary theory—namely the opposition between form and content—actually arises from a misconstruction of sign. When one interprets the internal relations of a sign system in Saussurean terms, the antithesis between form and content disappears.

Paull   Form and content are products of the misconstruction of signs?

David   Yes. If one begins with the role of thought in the sign and sign system, there ceases to be a point at which one can separate meaning and expression, or content and form.

The importance of the Saussurean theory only fully emerges when one reassesses traditional questions about human communication in terms of the Saussurean concepts. Many of these traditional questions—like the form/content issue—take on a new meaning, or cease to be coherent.

Paull   Your point is here that thought does not make use of signs, so to speak; rather thought is always inherent in signs

22

themselves. I think I am still at a stage, however, when some reiteration and application would help. What was the famous illustration which you just mentioned?

David It has to do with the concepts of SIGNIFICATION and VALUE. I have described them as one of the sets of paradoxical terms in Saussurean theory. These two terms are, in fact, of the essence in understanding a system of relations. Now Saussure illustrated these terms by considering money:

Return to 'value' and 'arbitrariness'

> To determine what a five-franc piece is worth one must therefore know: (1) that it can be exchanged for a fixed quantity of a different thing, e.g. bread; and (2) that it can be compared with a similar value of the same system, e.g. a one-franc piece, or with coins of another system (a dollar, etc.). In the same way a word can be exchanged for something dissimilar, an idea; besides, it can be compared with something of the same nature, another word. Its value is therefore not fixed so long as one simply states that it can be 'exchanged' for a given concept, i.e. that it has this or that signification: one must also compare it with similar values, with other words that stand in opposition to it. Its content is really fixed only by the concurrence of everything that exists outside it. Being part of a system, it is endowed not only with a signification but also and especially with a value, and this is something quite different.

Saussure, p. 115

He goes on to exemplify this through the French word *mouton*: while it has the same signification as English *sheep*, it does not have the same value, since, when English speakers discuss meat to be served, they use a second term—*mutton*—which does not exist in the French system.

Now when one extrapolates from this small example to a whole linguistic system, the difficulties of calibrating two systems are obvious. While it often seems a straightforward matter to connect terms of similar signification across languages, establishing similar values is another matter again. One has to remember, of course, that, across two languages, meanings with affinities of signification may be realised by very different aspects of the total system. So a meaning associated with a grammatical category like tense in English, may be expressed, in Chinese say, by a class of words (in combination with a signal of completeness, or aspect).

Paull It would seem then that there are far greater problems in translating and comparing two different languages, or more widely two different cultures. I can see that, by focusing on the significations—the *mouton* to *sheep* relations—it might look as if two systems were alike. However, if the values aren't comparable then the focus on signification has distorted the comparison.

David Precisely. And this looks back to the short discussion we had on continuity and change in child language development.

Paull Well, I can see many situations of relevance for this point. We have often mentioned Whorf and the theory of linguistic relativity—and I gather you wish to focus on this work in a

Whorf's Theory of linguistic relativity, in John B. Carroll (ed.), *Language, Thought and Reality*, MIT Press, Massachusetts, 1976 later discussion. In the debates surrounding linguistic relativity, it is value which rarely gets mentioned.

David   Yes. If one takes the arguments of the philosopher Max Black as an example, one can see that Whorf's critics are preoccupied with significations and unaware of the far-reaching consequences of considering values.

With such an emphasis, it is little wonder that Black comes to the conclusions he does concerning the relationship between language and the experiences of different communities.

M. Black, 'Some troubles with Whorfianism, in S. Hook (ed.), *Language and Philosophy*, New York U.P., New York, 1969

Paull   Okay. He says that 'no roads lead from grammar to metaphysics'. I take it, this means language does not directly determine one's world view.

David   When one focuses on signification only, it is inevitable that the differences between two meaning systems will be neutralised. This is because the act of arguing for a difference of signification can always be turned around and used against the idea of relativity. It can always be counter claimed: 'Oh well, you have just explained the special character of the meaning from language x, and since we are not speaking language x, but English, it is clear that the meaning can be expressed in English'.

Paull   I think Black himself uses this argument, doesn't he?

David   As you noted earlier, I am planning to look at the specific issues relevant to linguistic relativity after we survey some actual differences between cultures and patterns of meaning. At this point we are just trying to clarify the place of thought within a consistent theory of signs. It is worth adding, however, had attention been given to the concept of value the whole character of the Whorfian debate would have been different.

Paull   How do you explain the bias towards signification, then?

concepts of value and signification, Saussure, p. 111 and following

David   Well value, first of all, is a more difficult concept in that traditional accounts of language do not prepare us for it. Signification on the other hand seems to parallel the standard accounts of reference or naming—although it is, of course, very, very different when seen in its Saussurean context.

Saussure himself gave special emphasis to value, as well as to what he called the 'radical arbitrariness' of signs. This last point means that there is no natural connection between, say, a concept SIGNIFIED and the slice of sound SIGNIFIER that is bonded to it—in other words, the relationship is purely conventional.

Saussure's emphasis is very revealing. It helps to bring out the social/collective basis of language: 'it exists only by virtue of a sort of contract signed by the members of a community'.

Saussure, p. 14

The arbitrary nature of the sign explains in turn why the social fact alone can create a linguistic system. The community is necessary if values that owe their existence solely to usage and general acceptance are to be set up; by himself the individual is incapable of fixing a single value.

Saussure, p. 113

Paull This issue of value and the social 'contract' explains one of your earlier references to Wittgenstein. You mentioned Wittgenstein's attack on the idea of a private language.

David Well Wittgenstein attacked the notion of a private language; and he also emphasised that statements about our subjective experiences depend for their meaning on the public criteria of linguistic behaviour. I see, then, a congruence between Wittgenstein's overall attack on the idea of private meanings and Saussure's earlier insights into value, arbitrariness, and the social contract of language.

Paull The drift of your various arguments might be stated in the following way: when trying to describe a system of communication one begins in the community and arrives at the individual; not the other way round.

David I suppose that's an appropriate generalisation.

Paull Now, we have considered the Saussurean theory with respect to a range of intellectual issues: phonology, life sciences, developmental studies, code, form and content, linguistic relativity, reference, the question of a private language.

I know you have not said all you wish to say on those matters. But have we dealt with all we need to consider on the place of thought in a theory of the sign? Because it seems to me that we need to focus our global discussion now. This could be done by looking at the activity of analysis through some examples. Perhaps we need to examine how one grapples with units in various combinations.

David That's right. Saussure offers a further set of terms which enables one to examine how the various relations in a language function. The two terms, according to Saussure, correspond to different forms of our mental activity. Hence, they are pertinent to the question of thought in a theory of signs.

The terms are also important tools for analysing particular configurations and combinations of signs.

Paull I imagine you're referring to SYNTAGMATIC and PARADIGMATIC relations. They are certainly terms used widely across disciplines; and you mentioned them only briefly yourself.

David Yes. Their application is very wide. The SYNTAGMATIC RELATIONS reflect the linearity of language. The chain of succession in speech creates an opposition between a term and 'everything that precedes or follows it, or to both'. If we take the words of the clause below, we can see that each word creates a contrast with the other 'terms' in the 'effective series'. Let's focus on the word *world*.

Syntagm and paradigm

Saussure, p. 123

'Solid shapes are prominent in the world of young children'.

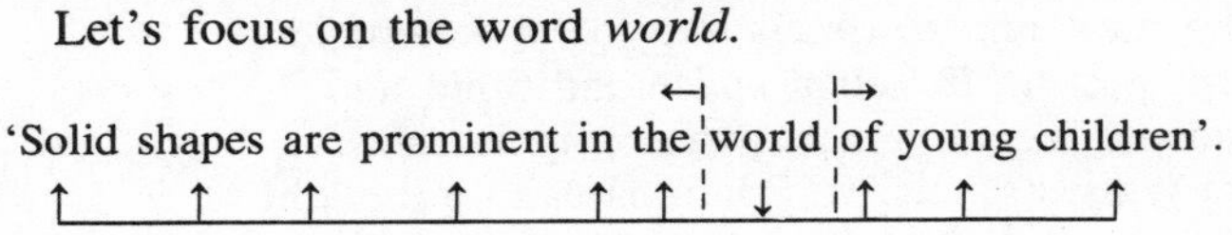

Figure 4

25

The arrows suggest the 3 kinds of opposition involved: what's gone before ← what comes after →; and both of these together ⌐⌐. This 'co-ordination' of terms can be referred to as a syntagm.

Paull   Okay; in the syntagm, one has a fixed succession of terms.

David   Well. . .they're fixed in so much as they are there—they are actually terms in a discourse; and their places relative to one another determine values or functions.

The other kind of relations don't occur in the discourse: they are the stock of terms which have something in common with the term in the syntagm but which are **not** in the syntagm themselves. In short they are all the forms of associative relation between a term and the stored memory of the speaker. Saussure actually called these latter relations 'associative'—the word 'paradigmatic' is now more common, however.

To illustrate associative relations Saussure offers the following diagram of the French word *enseignement: teaching*.

Figure 5

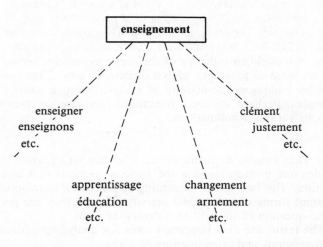

Saussure, p. 126

Saussure, p. 126

One can see from this schema of associative relations, why Saussure saw a word as a centre in a 'constellation': it is the point of convergence of an 'indefinite number of co-ordinated terms'.

Paull   Does Saussure have an illustration of the differences between these two types of relations—something like the money analogy in the discussion of value?

David   Yes he does: think of a building with, say, a row of Doric columns. Now the relationship between a column and its achitrave, the roof, and so on, is like the syntagmatic relations—it is present in actual space and time; and it involves different kinds of functions across a configuration.

illustration of the difference between syntagm and associative relations, Saussure, p. 124

By contrast, the associative relations can be thought of as being like the possibility of Ionic or Corinthian columns etc. . . . These relations are not present in the configuration—they are *in absentia*.

This contrast brings out the fact that a syntagm involves a fixed number of elements and an order of succession. Associative (paradigmatic) relations are neither fixed in number nor in the order by which they arise in the mind of the speaker.

Paull   These difficulties are what Saussure must have meant by the terms corresponding to different forms of our mental activity. What do you think?

David   Yes. The claim is one of Saussure's more enigmatic and less elaborated observations. Let's reflect on how the syntagmatic and the paradigmatic involve different aspects of thinking.

Roman Jakobson & Morris Halle, *Fundamentals of Language*, Mouton & Co.'s, Gravenhage, 1956

Paull   Well, I recall that these two terms have been used in discussing aphasia.

David   Yes. Roman Jakobson suggested that aphasias might be characterised in terms of the loss of either one or the other of these two kinds of relation. I am not in a position to assess the present status of this idea. Still it brings us again to the question of different modes of mental activity.

Paull   It seems to me that these two kinds of relations have different implications. For example, syntagmatic relations could be stated in rules—in other words, they could be more easily formalised. But how could one formalise associative relations? There is an indefinite number of ways by which associations may be created. There is no principle by which their order can be established. It would follow, I think, that associative relations cannot be brought into a description of the language—at least a description which brings out the systematicity which you have stressed through the Saussurean approach.

David   The notion of rule is not, for me, a very helpful metaphor in the description of a language. Nevertheless, I take your point concerning formalisation. I would only like to add two observations concerning the reciprocal relation between the syntagmatic and the paradigmatic. (Let's stick to this term, instead of associative shall we?)

As with signification and value, the terms syntagm and paradigm ultimately produce a paradox, though again, an extremely helpful paradox! First of all, let's continue to think of words as the rank of the grammar with which we are working.

Ultimately, the separation between syntagm and paradigm becomes hard to make. Note that the constellation of a word's paradigmatic relations includes the word's characteristics of combination—its syntagmatic potential. So too, a syntagm needs to take account of specific paradigmatic possibilities; and without the paradigmatic relations, one would not be able even to recognise the units of the syntagm.

Paull   If I have got this situation straight, you are emphasising that the specific paradigmatic choice determines the syntagmatic combination; and the syntagmatic combination determines what parts of the paradigm are relevant. This is, in fact, much like the signification/value interdependence.

David It is one more of a number of relationships of mutual definition: signifié/signifiant; signification/value; syntagm/paradigm.

Now it may be clearer why I was not happy about the syntagm being described by rules. A syntagm is not autonomous: that is, it is not independent of paradigms.

Paull I note that you mentioned syntagms and paradigmatic relations in our discussion of the classroom. From what you have now brought out about those concepts, it's clearer to me that they do not constitute a simple 'slot and filler' relationship. Nevertheless I'm sure they have a place in clarifying structure in the processes of schooling.

There is one thing I would like to do now, at the end of our first discussion. I will try to offer you a synopsis of the Saussurean perspective; in particular, how Saussure's insights have affected your orientation to the relationship between language and thought.

David Yes, that sounds like a good strategy.

Paull Now, from my jottings I think I can enumerate a series of points by which the Saussurean approach can be characterised.

Summary

1 To understand the concept of a sign one has to understand the concept of a semiotic system; a language is not an aggregate of individual names or acts of reference.

2 A semiotic system is based on relationships of contrast or opposition: all units are negatively defined; therefore no sign can be addressed except in the context of its system.

3 The place of a sign in the system has to be considered in the light of two dichotomies: signification/value; and paradigmatic/syntagmatic relations.

4 The two terms within each of these dichotomies have a paradoxical interdependence; and this can be seen within the sign since the concept and the acoustic image (in language) cannot be separated.

5 Following from these points: a language always involves thought: thought is inherent in the very structure of the sign; similarly, one cannot conceive of thought except in the terms of a semiotic system—a community, public, system for meaning. So we might express it thus:

Figure 6

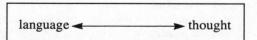

28

David Yes. If I can break in here. Your point (5) is fundamental to our continuing discussions. It takes us back to the quote from Saussure. . ..

Paull Wait. I know the one you have in mind: 'Thought, chaotic by nature, has to become ordered in the process of its decomposition'.

Saussure, p. 112

David It's an interesting paradox again, isn't it—that something only becomes ordered through decomposition?

Paull The five points I've mentioned imply that both language and thought must be viewed interactionally and collectively; certainly not in personal or individual terms only.

David My reasons for presenting these abstract considerations early in our discussions are probably clearer now. For me, coming to grips with the Saussurean concepts marked a re-organisation of my interpretations and perceptions of experience. I suppose I was a bit like the child who went from number operations to algebra—it was like being given a tool of which one could previously conceive only vaguely, if at all.

   My feelings are more emphatic in that the implications of Saussure's theory require a great deal of investigation and application. There is a commonly heard catchery that we are now in a 'post-structuralist era'. I find that ridiculous. It could only be uttered by a person who has not taken the trouble to confront the issues we've discussed. In fact, so much needs to be thought through.

Paull I certainly agree that the Saussurean concepts imply a total revision in how we talk about language.

David I only hope that you find them worth the effort.

Paull Well, we'll see. Now its your plan, isn't it, to move away from the abstractions of language and thought and towards the actual—communities 'talking and thinking'. . .?

The role of talking in the thinking of a community

Objectivity and learning

Paull One of the implications of our previous discussion, it seems to me, can be stated as a general point concerning method in the human sciences. In science it is always the objective view which is esteemed. I suppose the very essence of 'methodology' could be thought of as finding a means by which 'objectivity' is created. This is to say one needs to be able to address a phenomenon as if it were a thing, with 'thing-ish' qualities: with determinate boundaries, and with specific consequences in some causal scheme. It is this kind of conception of study that makes us isolate variables and set up experiments. There are many aspects of human research, however, in which this canonical approach does not seem possible. And language, from the Saussurean perspective, seems to be one such area.

David I'd want to take you up on this point, Paull, both with respect to your last point concerning research into language, and also how our previous discussion bears on questions of methodology.

Paull Well, just let me elaborate on my own experiences in psychology and education.

First of all, in the various fields of my study and teaching, I have typically been both observer and participant at one and the same time. This seems to me a crucial point—it complicates and relativises all the areas of my professional work.

It is perhaps easiest to see in my present counselling training and practice. On the one hand I am learning about counselling by doing it; and on the other, I am learning about particular individuals through their coming to know me.

David Okay. I see that this is a highly involved situation. It is not likely, for instance, that the kind of 'knowledge' which you develop could be presented as specifications. All your experience has to be seen 'in relation to' a complex of factors.

Paull Exactly. But this is not different, qualitatively or quantitatively, from the situations I've experienced in teaching. In a classroom, a teacher is interacting with each individual; one can view the relationship one to one as well as one to many. In fact, as a teacher, your perspective has to be double most of the time, i.e. picking up or monitoring each individual as well as integrating the discourse of the whole class. This is not to imply that the teacher's role should be directive. I mean merely that the teacher is always a participator—the educational process cannot be addressed as thing-ish in any of its aspects. Hence, it is so difficult to describe the 'good' teacher in absolute terms. . . . And so it goes with respect to methods, objectives, curriculum . . .

In teaching, then, one never has the luxury of an outside view — the objective approach. Does this, perhaps, help to explain why there is such pluralism in educational theory; psycho-analytic theory; sociology; and human sciences in general? Is there an analogy between the situation I outlined in education and the study of languages in their cultural context?

David   Well, there is. But let me add that there is an analogy not just with linguistics but right across many disciplines. This was one point that did begin to emerge in our previous discussion.

Even if we begin outside the human-social sciences, in physics say, the 'relativisation' of what can and can't be known is evident. In the writings of physicists like Heisenberg and Wheeler, one finds highly philosophical rejections of the objectivity in physics. For such physicists the cosmos is inherently participatory—much, I suppose, as we said thought was inherent in language. Even Niels Bohr himself spoke of the way there was an analogy between the role of the anthropologist (going into an alien community and observing) and the situation of the modern physicists (having to intervene in subatomic events in order to take measurements and know the state of the system). So we should not overlook this character of research in general. Objectivity, in an absolute sense, is not the luxury of any research.

Paull   Yes. But don't you feel that individual perspectives impinge more in certain forms of study?

David   Well, why don't we go to your other point: is linguistics a participatory study in the sense you outlined above? And furthermore, do Saussurean concepts help in describing a system which we cannot address as an object?

Paull   It is relevant to be clearer on these questions. For instance, when a teacher is making a judgment with respect to a child, the language of the child is a big factor in determining the teacher's judgment. Eltis has found, in fact, that it takes precedence over every other factor.

But the teacher is not interpreting the child's talk in an objective way—the teacher is not outside the system. As a member of numerous sub-groups across the community, the teacher's own talk must affect the evaluations she or he will make. Don't you agree?

W. Heisenberg, *Physics and Philosophy*, Harper and Row, N.Y., 1962

J. A. Wheeler, 'Law without law', in P. Medawar and J. H. Shelley (eds.), *Structure in Science and Art*, Excerpta Medica, Amsterdam, 1980

N. Bohr, *Atomic Physics and Human Knowledge*, Interscience/John Wiley, New York, 1963

Meanings and actions: Malinowski

David I'm trying to keep the threads of our conversation interwoven; and I think the points concerning objectivity, 'participatory' disciplines, and teacher/student language can all be treated by reflecting on semantics: namely, the branch of linguistics concerned with the study of meaning. Certainly, one cannot study a language from the outside! Let this be the first issue we examine. This is the objectivity issue, of course. Saussure makes another helpful point in this regard: note how, if you overhear speakers of a language which you yourself don't understand, then you will hear their utterances, more or less, as continuous. On the other hand, when you understand the system of that language, the utterances are actually heard as discrete units, as words. So, to identify the units of a language one has to be able to decode its meanings.

But let's ask ourselves what is required to decode the meanings of a community.

Paull In the first place one has to have a dictionary, a lexicon of some kind. Not a written one maybe, but certainly a 'wordhoard', as I think the early Anglo-Saxons use to call their memory of language.

David Certainly, a lexicon may be important. But there are a number of problems here. Depending on the kind of language, the actual forms of words can change considerably. To get some idea of this, think of looking up *was* in an English dictionary. First pretend, of course, that you do not know the language already: its variations of forms, and consistencies of function etc.

Paull The conclusion is, then, that one needs grammatical knowledge and some familiarity with the sound of the language?

David That would be the general view, wouldn't it? And many linguists would hold that view. But I think that it is quite inadequate: from knowing the words and grammar and sound system of a language it does not automatically follow that one can make sense in that language.

What seems essential to decoding the meanings of a community is that one be aware of the significant contexts in that culture.

Paull What do you mean 'significant contexts'?

David Briefly, the activities and goals around which the community is organised.

Paull It is simply then, the behaviour of the community.

David Well, as long as you include in behaviour, not just physical actions, but the purposes which direct the community. Also important are the conditions under which these purposes are pursued.

Paull All this seems a bit vague or, at least, abstract.

David Well, the relevant name on this point is Malinowski. In his study of the Trobriand Islanders it became clear to Malinowski that relying on dictionaries and grammar was misleading. You see, the dictionaries were themselves organised on the principle of 'find the nearest English word for the word in question'. Malinowski offers a short text as illustration. Translated word for word, it comes out as:

This is also discussed by Halliday, in M. A. K. Halliday & Ruqaiya Hasan, *Language, Context and Text: Aspects of Language in a Social-Semiotic Perspective*, Oxford University Press, 1989.

we run	front-wood	ourselves
we paddle	in place;	we turn we see
companion ours;	he runs	rear-wood
behind	their sea-arm	Pilolu

Malinowski shows just how many linguistic and cultural details need to be elaborated in order to interpret this brief text. We probably shouldn't recount the full range, but essentially, one is confronted here with a boasting speech referring to canoes and a time of overseas trading. The speaker is gloating over the superiority of his canoe. And much of the meaning is lost, we are told, without an understanding of the nature of competition in the tribal psychology—its ceremonies and commerce.

B. Malinowski, in C. K. Ogden & I. A. Richards, *The Meaning of Meaning*, Routledge & Kegan Paul, London, 1949, pp. 300–1

   Special features of the linguistic system (e.g. the use of the possessive pronoun: *their sea-arm Pilolu*) consistently lead the investigator back to the culture in general. Malinowski concluded:

> Instead of translating, of inserting simply an English word for a native one, we are faced by a long and not altogether simple process of describing wide fields of custom, of social psychology and of tribal organisation which correspond to one term or another. We see that linguistic analysis inevitably leads us into the study of all the subjects covered by Ethnographic field-work.

Malinowski, pp. 301–2

Paull   Well the points Malinowski makes seem overstated if I refer to my own experience of travel. Doesn't one's shared humanness give a basic understanding in these matters? Can't we rely, somewhat, on cultural universals?

David   Malinowski's comments do arise in his study of what he calls 'primitive languages'. He contrasts the European languages, and their forms of reflective discourse, with more primitive uses of language. He finds that the reflective uses are 'far-fetched and derivative'. Malinowski claims that the central character of languages is as 'a mode of action and not an instrument of reflection'. This view emphasises the role of language in 'practical action' and as a 'link in concerted human activity, as a piece of human behaviour'.

Malinowski, p. 312

Malinowski, p. 312

   So Malinowski's comparison appears to be between a technological/reflective orientation and a primitive/pragmatic tradition. But I think all that is at issue here is greater or lesser contrasts between cultures being compared. Obviously we are more likely to notice the significance of cultural contexts when we are amidst conventions which are very different from our own. The role of context in the analyses of meaning, however, is constant. It's visibility as a factor in analysis merely varies depending on who's doing the looking (the analysis) and what it is they happen to be examining.

Paull   I can certainly see how this last point could escape notice, given the fact that the Trobriand Islanders probably sent very few linguists and ethnographers to London and New York! The habits of the dominant culture always become the baseline in ethnographic description.

Meaning in Malagasy

Edward Louis Keenan & Elinor Ochs, 'Becoming a competent speaker of Malagasy', in Timothy Shopen (ed.), *Languages and Their Speakers*, Winthrop Publishers, Massachusetts, 1979, p. 138

David   No doubt. And this takes us back to the earlier points concerning objectivity and the participation of the analyst. A short study by Keenan and Ochs exemplifies the main points of our discussion so far. Their description of Malagasy (a language of Madagascar) is presented in two parts. The first part reviews the production of 'sentences' and matters related to that special idealisation that we call 'the language system'. One of the central technical matters with which they are concerned is the function of subject in Malagasy. After this half of their paper, the writers reiterate a point they made at the outset of their study: namely, that knowing the words, grammar, and sounds of the language will not make a European a 'competent speaker' of Malagasy. Even with the 'linguistic' knowledge, a European visitor to Madagascar would 'still find himself unable to perform successfully most social acts requiring the use of speech. . .'.

Paull   What is the obstruction here? Is it that one needs to know specific points related to canoes, fishing nets or whatever else has a bearing upon the day to day activities?

David   No, the difficulties relate to interpersonal meanings which affect the whole system of the culture. Let me, perhaps, list these in a summary way, offer an example from the anecdotes of Keenan and Ochs, and then proceed to the general methodological conclusions the writers draw from their experience.
   The crucial behavioural norms relate to:
1   the status of news, or new information, in the relatively closed peasant community;
2   the indirectness of orders and requests;
3   the collective nature of responsibility in the initiation of any action.
4   the avoidance of the display of individual abilities (ie. abilities over and above those of one's equals);
5   the avoidance of 'shame', closely related to non-committalism and the avoidance of confrontations.

Paull   And you don't feel these norms are evident in our communities too?

David   Keenan and Ochs note how hard it is to bring out the way these 'conditions on the use of speech' affect behaviour systematically. They noted, for instance, how a group of boys came to visit them. They were acquaintances of the writers. After about 20 minutes of talk, conversation moved to the topic of cut feet. Eventually, from the back of the group a boy came forward to exhibit his severely bleeding foot. All of the proceedings—the

34

oblique introduction of the 'request' for help; the presence of the group of peers; the place of the hurt boy in the background— were conventional in a community which would be appalled by explicit, individual requests, particularly on one's own behalf.

In a related way, Keenan and Ochs could not give a bicycle to one of their informants who walked for hours to school—it would have been a gift he could not easily share; hence, the bike would have differentiated him in a strongly egalitarian milieu. So too, with European-styled schooling: if one child had done a homework assignment, he would naturally give it to all the children to use and copy. One can only imagine what might be the consequences of the title 'outstanding pupil'.

Paull   What were the conclusions Keenan and Ochs drew with respect to objectivity?

David   Yes. They emphasise this point. They note various kinds of understanding they would have missed had they merely commuted to the village. But mainly, they argue that the quality of observation will be conditioned, for a visitor, by the 'role he occupies in the local social structure'. By considering this place in the social structure, he can 'judge what distortion his very presence introduces into the range of phenomena he will be trying to observe and understand'.

Keenan & Ochs, p. 157

Keenan & Ochs, p. 157

Paull   So, we are back at objectivity and observation.

David   Yes we are. But Keenan and Ochs exemplify these issues and the issues raised in Malinowski's seminal paper. One never escapes the need to include context in a description of meanings—our perception of the need merely changes depending on who is doing the description and which language is being described.

Still, before moving away from the Malagasy example, I think it's important to recall that the Keenan and Ochs study had two distinct sections—the linguistic and the ethnographic. While the linguistic section was, we can say, systematic, the ethnographic material relevant to the conditions of speaking was not systematic. The overall study was not integrated in its descriptive methods.

Paull   It seems as if linguistics has its own constellation of sub-disciplines: phonology, syntax, semantics, context. These all appear to have their own separate methods and problems. Isn't this division of language much like the divisions which we have criticised in psychology—for instance, the separation of cognition and affect?

David   Yes, I have to concede the accuracy of the comparison. Formalisation and idealisation have produced, across some schools of linguistics, a tendency to address language as if it were a bundle of autonomous components. I think it is accurate to say, however, that ultimately all branches of linguistics have to refer to meaning in order to develop the descriptions offered by their particular level of analysis. So, one finds in linguistics a corroboration of the view we have discussed with respect to human psychology: namely, that a phenomenon which has been broken into parts must also be viewed back together as a whole.

The British linguist J.R. Firth expressed the situation with the metaphor of light passing through a glass prism. Language is like the white light and the process of analysis is represented by the prism: the prism disperses the unitry character of the light into various strands of the spectrum—various levels of analysis. These are like the separate levels of abstraction at which the linguist works.

I recall you mentioning, Paull, that divisions often lead to theories which give primacy to one or other aspect of an analysis. When Chomsky's theories gave a special status to syntax, it was thought by many linguists that this branch of linguistics could be conducted autonomously. This proved not to be the case—considerations of meaning had to be introduced. And I think this need to defer to meaning should have been evident to anyone who reviewed the function of language in society; and to any linguist who thought closely about Saussure's theory of signs.

Paull Well, you are certainly filling out my understanding of linguistics, at least with respect to general intellectual issues: methods; objectivity and so on. But are we getting closer to the relation between talking and thinking?

David Yes, I think we are. From some of the topics discussed so far, our progress can be seen:

1 objectivity;
2 participation and observation;
3 complexity and relativity in the roles of a teacher;
4 contexts and the description of meaning.

Meta-language: two routes to universalism

David Now a consistent theme in our present talk has been the idea of a META-LANGUAGE. We haven't yet used the term; but our main concerns have been with the description of phenomena in which meanings are already involved. Hence, our difficulties must relate, at least in part, to the problem of using a system of meanings to describe a system of meanings! It is important to keep this problem in mind as we try to discuss the dependency between talking and knowledge.

Paull So, a meta-language is essentially a language for the description of language . . .? The point of our discussion so far, it seems to me, is to clarify the relativity inherent in the description of cultures, whether one begins at the linguistic system or not. I can see the basis for this relativism: every act of description will be actually a form of reaction between the system of the ethnographer and the system being studied.

What about the attempts to break out from this relativism? I know, for example, that various semantic theories have emphasised universals rather than differences. What is the status of work which makes use of formal descriptions to get at universal aspects of meaning?

David Let's look briefly then at the recent efforts to formalise semantics. If you believe, as Chomsky does, that there is an innate language faculty which has an organisation specific enough to be characterised as a universal grammar, then it is a short step to a universalist semantics. In fact, one does not even have to come via this route. One might, for instance, begin at the belief that the world happens to have a certain structure, no matter who is perceiving it, and that the business of language is to mirror that structure. This is the general character of Russell's approach, as I understand it. An interesting aspect of this latter route is an impatience with natural languages. Russell displays this. It is as if one should not be able to say 'the king of France is bald' when there is no king of France—at least, all 'errors' of truth, illogicality, and vagueness should be evident from the logical form of the language. So Russell's approach has been   Watling, p. 76
likened to a search for a perfect grammar, that is a grammar that would not mislead us about the structure of the external world.

Much of this, I know Paull, you are familiar with yourself. But it is important to emphasise how direct a route there is from either Chomsky or Russell to universalism. Whether one begins with innatism or the idea that reality is given, it is close to implicit that human experience will have boundaries or limits. Expressed in terms of meanings this can be said as, 'There will be a given semantic space, and although different cultures may arrange their systems of meanings in diverse ways, overall there will have to be considerable correspondences between the meanings of one culture and the meanings of any other'.

Paull This takes us back to cognitive meanings, doesn't it? The view that some meanings are the core or essential meanings?

David Yes. The approach was particularly evident throughout linguistics in three ways.

Firstly, during the heyday of transformational grammar (TG)—the late 1960s—it was claimed by proponents of TG that the rules by which one could turn one sentence into another systematically related sentence (e.g. an active sentence into its passive form) were 'meaning preserving'. This is to say, applying the transformational rule did not change the fundamental meaning of the sentence. This was an aspect of the theory of autonomous syntax, mentioned earlier.

Paull I take it this point about meaning preserving rules has undergone change.

David That's right. But maybe we shouldn't stop to examine this quite now. The second point concerning cognitive meaning is more general.

Secondly, it has been a hope of some linguists that semantic description could be rendered in a formal, even axiomatic, fashion. There seemed to be some reason for this hope. First of all logic as a subject was developing, particularly in its handling of 'adverbial' expressions (eg. specifications of time). Furthermore, many linguists were themselves making language look more like the study of propositions, more like logic. It should be noted, of course, that these remarks do not apply to the functionalist and sociological traditions of linguistics.

The third point relates to both the first and the second: various models were proposed whereby a 'semantic component' could mediate between the syntactic and phonological components. A method was introduced here from anthropology—the idea of analysing into components or features. These features were placed in square brackets to indicate that they stood for abstract components of meaning [+ animate], [+ male]. It has been common to regard these components as universal—as we mentioned in our previous discussion of atomism.

Paull   I think I see where you are heading. Beginning with your third or last point: no matter whether the components are placed in brackets, or written in capitals, they are still words of the natural language, English. This is to say they have particular significations and values in the system of an existing language.

David   Yes. We can pretend, of course, that they stand for aspects of reality. But it is always **our** reality as speakers of English.

Paull   The same applies to logical, artificial languages—your second point. Or does it? Doesn't logic stand outside language? and therefore provide a meta-language, or a base for one at least?

David   With regard to the second point the concept of a semiotic system is helpful. We can assume, like Russell, that logic will set us free from the obfuscations of English, Chinese, Russian etc. But we must face the fact that developments in logic and mathematics occur within particular socio-cultural contexts. They do not occur randomly across the human race. They are forms of discourse which, like all forms of discourse, require the participation of groups with shared goals and elaborate traditions. In short, formal languages (like the developments in logic and mathematics) constitute semiotic systems within cultural traditions which may not coincide with the boundaries of natural languages. Still, mathematics and logic have evolved—their presence in a culture depends on certain preceding conditions.

Paull   Well . . . it's plain that a term like *animate* must be interpreted according to culture . . . I wouldn't have thought of it as a strong candidate for an inventory of universal semantic features. But *male* and *female* are different. Given that I probably favour [+ female] as against [+ male], the distinction does seem to me more plausible as a universal. Still, I take your point that they **are** words of English.

David   Yes [+ male] is often cited as a universal, as one of the simple binary oppositions which works across languages or cultures. But again a Saussurean concept clarifies the matter: if one refers only to signification, the universals appear to be a useful shorthand—one could imagine them having a role in an information storage machine, one which had to disambiguate lexical items, either in decoding or encoding.

38

But if one recalls the concept of value, as described by Saussure, the whole status of male/female is modified. The place of these words in the Anglo-American-Australian culture differs greatly by comparison with, say, traditional Aboriginal cultures in Australia.

As soon as value is considered, it becomes clear that the universal components are illusory. The description becomes a matter of alternative perspectives: do we make an Australian Aboriginal term the component for the description of English? What about the speakers of Malagasy—is it correct to see their behaviour, as some Europeans have, as covert and even devious? Or, on the other hand, should we adopt a Malagasy perspective, in which Europeans can seem astonishingly direct, brash, and self-preoccupied?

Paull   Now it strikes me that you have been preparing the ground for something beyond componential analysis and Malagasy. What point are we at in our attack on talking and thinking?

David   You're right. Our discussion, from objectivity to context and semantic universals, has been necessary to the assessment of the main work I wish to examine in this discussion.

You'll recall the references I made in our previous discussion to the Central Asian study, conducted by Vygotsky and Luria during the collectivisation program of 1931−32. That investigation in itself provided opportunities to examine most of the issues we have discussed to date. So, let's look over that material, the intentions of the researchers, the adequacy of the methods used, and the significance the research could have for our discussions of sign systems and behaviour.

Paull   As I recall your brief sketch of the study; you emphasised two points:
1   that processes of cognition are themselves dependent upon socio-cultural practices; or, more generally,
2   that aspects of mental life, which have been regarded as the universal conditions of thought, are actually products of the community's experience.

David   Luria has expressed these issues in the following way:

> During the course . . . of psychology's attempt to make itself an exact science, it has looked for laws of mental activity "within the organism". It has regarded association, or apperception, the structural nature of perception, or conditioned reflexes underlying behaviour as either natural and unchanging properties of the organism (physiological psychology) or as manifestations or intrinsic properties of the mind (idealistic psychology). The notion that the intrinsic properties and laws of mental activity remain unchanging has also led to attempts to set up a positivist social psychology and sociology based on the premise that social activities display mental properties operating **within** individuals . . . [my emphasis]

For Luria, the problem was that, between the study of physiology on the one hand and the idealism on the other, an

Observers in Uzbekistan

A. R. Luria, *Cognitive Development, Its Cultural and Social Foundations*, (ed.) Michael Cole, Harvard University Press, USA, 1976, p. 4

adequate theory of human mental activity could not emerge. The physiology could not separate humans from animals, and the subjectivism could only describe without offering any explanation. 'Moreover, the laws of logical thought, active remembering, selective attention, and acts of the will in general, which form the basis for the most complex and characteristic higher forms of human mental activity, successfully resisted causal interpretation, and thus remained beyond the forefront of the progression of scientific thought'.

Luria, p. 5

Paull Did Vygotsky and Luria set out with a specific hypothesis? Or did they merely react to inadequacies in the behaviourist and mentalist traditions?

David Yes, they had a specific hypothesis; although their work in its present form seems more descriptive. Understanding their hypothesis depends on a knowledge of two concepts, however. So, I'll just define these before I state the hypothesis.

Luria refers to 'graphic-functional' experience and thinking by contrast to 'rational'. What is meant here is the difference between practices which are guided by the concrete features of the objects and situations confronted in day-to-day experience, and those activities of the mind which permit human beings to go beyond 'the data of direct sensory experience'. The graphic-functional is immediate and pragmatic; the rational can involve the creation of logical codes by which objects of thought (just as important as sensory experience) can be examined and discussed with 'the same objectivity as the data of direct sensory experience'.

Luria, p. 10

Luria, p. 10

Paull This distinction between direct-sensory and rational needs some further clarification. It seems to me like Popper's distinction between world 2 and world 3. Is that an accurate comparison?

K. Popper, *Objective Knowledge: An Evolutionary Approach*, Oxford University Press, Oxford, 1972.

David They are related, but different. As I recall, Popper divides reality into three worlds: world 1—the objects and phenomena of the external world; world 2—the psychological states that constitute our sense of primary experience; and world 3—the products of mind: the information which cultures store: forms of knowledge which have an 'exo-somatic' status. For example, nobody holds the table of logarithms in his or her head, but this product of human thinking is a cultural tool.

Luria, following Vygotsky, recognised the importance of cultural tools; and Popper's world 3 is, of course, relevant to their theories. But the Russians emphasised 'the semantic and system structure of consciousness'.

Luria, p. 11

Paull Well, couldn't that emphasis be described using Popper's terms: namely, world 2 is constantly undergoing restructuring due to its interactions with world 3. That is to say, my states of consciousness and mental experience are being reorganised through the use I make of the artefacts of cultural experience . . .?

David   Vygotsky certainly concentrated on the changes and developments in thinking. He noted, for instance, that a young child thinks by remembering while an adolescent remembers by thinking. You see, with the adolescent, social experience mediates through the ability to talk **in** to oneself just as one can talk **out** to the world. The semantic system of the community becomes the principal of **internal** organisation; and in such a way, the community meanings come to structure our going out to the world: our ideas of **external** reality. This again is a difficult notion. It is as if there is a kind of reciprocal delimitation between psychological experience and experience of the world, the kind of paradox we discussed with respect to the two halves of the sign.

Paull   I see your point here as a description of inter-subjectivity.

David   Yes. Beginning with the relationship between a mother and child, there is a consistent development whereby interaction encompasses more and more of the community's sense of what is salient. The inter-subjectivity takes on a kind of organic growth—the subjectivity evolves and reorganises as a result of wider 'inter'-action. Now for Luria and Vygotsky this development is a form of construction. Hence, mind has a material explanation in their approach. Popper, on the other hand, characterises himself as an interactionist. But here the word is not referring to social interaction. I take it to mean that it is mind and the material universe that interact. In fact one has interaction between the three worlds Popper discusses. But the ontogenesis of mind is not addressed in exclusively materialist terms. And the world 2—the world of psychological experience—is not viewed as a social construction; in particular, not as a reflection of socio-economic factors.

Paull   What was the hypothesis, then? I suppose it was hoped the graphic-functional and the rational could be both contrasted and related to one another?

David   Vygotsky and Luria wanted to examine 'the historical development of mental systems', just as the cognitive development of a child could be examined as he/she became an adolescent. The process of collectivisation in 1931—32 was probably unique in human history for the speed with which social change was introduced across diverse communities.

By entering the feudal social and economic conditions of Uzbekistan and Khirgizia, the researchers had the opportunity to witness communities coming to terms with 'new fields of knowledge' and 'new motives for action'. Cotton-growing and pastoralist communities suddenly became responsible for collective planning, evaluation, and modifications. Networks of schools made some small beginnings in communities 'virtually 100 per cent illiterate for centuries'. The place of women underwent dramatic change—Islam meant that many women knew only the *ichkari* (women's quarters).

Luria, p. 13

41

Paull So all the members of these communities were not at the same level with respect to abstractions and theorising? Working as a cotton grower is very different from being predominantly in the women's quarters.

David Well, the hypothesis tried to build in this kind of variation. Luria and Vygotsky 'hypothesised that people with a primarily graphic-functional reflection of reality would show a different system of mental process from people with a predominantly abstract, verbal, and logical approach to reality'.

Luria, p. 18

Now none of the subjects observed 'had in effect received any higher education'. But, as you point out, their practical experiences were different. The subjects were:

Luria, p. 14

1 *Ichkari* women (in remote villages; illiterate; cut off from social activities outside the women's quarters).
2 Peasants (in remote villages, illiterate, no contact with socialised labour).
3 Women teachers of kindergartens (no formal education or literacy training).
4 Collective farm workers and young people (who had taken only short courses).
5 Women students at teachers' school (low qualifications; perhaps two to three years of study).

Paull Group four is crucial to the study, I imagine. They would be the ones most involved in what you called new motives for action. They would be doing all the plans, keeping records, arguing policies, chairing meetings, and so on. . .

David Yes; all the groups three to five were open to the consequences of the new social order. In short, they were the ones most exposed to literacy, technology, and new kinds of social relations.

Paull What about the objectivity issue we have been treating as a theme in our present discussion? How did a team of Muscovite researchers control for their own impact in Uzbekistan?!

David Yes. Of course, a lot of attention needed to be directed to this aspect of the study. First of all, a great deal of the research was conducted in tea-houses, or situations in which it was conventional to spend time in relaxed conversation: exchanging opinions, discussing 'riddles', and so forth. Usually the subjects were encouraged not only to give an answer, but to work their way to an alternative answer as well. The discussions always involved more than one to one conversation and the problems posed always offered a number of solutions—at least graphic-functional and rational alternatives. An assistant, in the background, took down proceedings, and a 'clean copy' was made later. Luria points out that even a brief session would involve a half day of writing up.

Paull The only point that still needs to be classified is the nature of the problems discussed. Were measurements involved? Were the problems the same as might have been posed by researchers in other contexts?

David No. The questions discussed had to be meaningful in the context of research. This, combined with the openness of the problems, resulted in a qualitative approach to the data. The general areas of this qualitative approach included perception; generalisation; deduction and inference; problem-solving; imagination; and self-analysis.

Paull I see. They began with perception . . . and ultimately reached questions relating to self and imagination.

David Luria notes that one aim had been specifically to examine the Cartesian notion 'of the primacy of self-consciousness, with a secondary rank accorded to the perception of the external world and other people'. In contrast to the Cartesian approach they assumed that 'the perception of oneself results from the clear perception of others and [that] the processes of self-perception are shaped through social activity . . .'

Luria, p. 19

But we'll have a lot to say about this quotation. Let's begin with perception.

Paull It's not unusual for psychology texts to begin with perception as a topic. And the reasons for this have some bearing on our inter-disciplinary conversation.

David Yes. The place of perception studies in psychology is particularly relevant to our consideration of objectivity and of universals. How would you explain the significance perception studies have had for psychology?

Paull Well, of all the areas of study in the discipline, it was generally felt that, in the study of perception, the psychologists' function would be most like that of researchers in the physical sciences. I suppose it has always been an aim of the human and social sciences to produce models which would both describe and explain, which would permit predictions to be made, which would be free of indeterminacies and so on. . . In short, it was assumed that perception involved mechanisms which were common to all human beings. As such, aspects of these mechanisms might be measured and examined free of subjectivity, much as it was thought other experimental sciences were conducted.

David Now if we concentrate on visual perception, one can identify the basis for the expectations you mention. The optical mechanism appears to have some analogy with a camera. But this analogy is fundamentally misleading.

Seeing and syllogisms

Paull I agree. I think one has to go far beyond the analogy of a camera. The analogy fails to convey the place of interpretation in the process of vision.

David The situation is encapsulated in Richard Gregory's title: *The Intelligent Eye*. He shows, through experiments based on visual paradoxes and 'impossible' objects, that 'perceiving is a kind of thinking'. It involves problem-solving, interpretation, and the construction of models of an external world. Gregory calls these

R. L. Gregory, *The Intelligent Eye*, McGraw-Hill, New York, p. 59

Gregory, p. 86

models 'object hypotheses'. Perception makes 'remarkably efficient use of strictly inadequate, and so ambiguous, information for selecting internally stored hypotheses of the current state of the external world'.

Paull   A crucial characteristic of Gregory's view is the degree to which perception is heuristic: the degree to which it has an 'as if' quality.

David   Certainly there is a considerable distance between the 'hypotheses' to which Gregory refers and the kind of simple correspondence which is implicit in, say, Bertrand Russell's idea of 'knowledge by acquaintance'. Just as perception has been of special interest to psychologists, visual perception has a unique role in the philosophical tradition.

Paull   Well, I recall you mentioning that many philosophers had been well known in their day for treatises on optics—Déscartes, for example.

David   The point goes much deeper. It is best clarified by Richard Rorty in his *Philosophy and the Mirror of Nature*. Rorty examines the ways in which philosophical enquiry has been drawn to the metaphors of the eye, seeing, and to the idea of reflecting nature through linguistic or logical relations.

The 'radical arbitrariness of the 2 parts of the sign' also re-emerges as an issue. For, at the centre of debates about perception just as at the centre of arguments concerning language, there is a desire to base human knowledge on something other than convention. What Saussure's arbitrariness tells us is that language is conventional . . . not random, but conventional. Now Rorty goes back to Greek philosophy, to Parmenides and Plato, in order to bring out the historical connection between vision, reflection, and 'correspondence to reality'.

Richard Rorty,
*Philosophy and the
Mirror of Nature*,
Basil Blackwell,
Oxford, 1980,
pp. 130—1

> . . . we can see the history of epistemology and semantics as the attempt to 'ground' predicative discourse on a nonconventional relation to reality. Such a grounding will divide predicative discourse into two parts, one corresponding to the Way of Truth, because 'anchored' epistemologically or semantically by unmediated relationships, and the other corresponding to the Way and Opinion . . . it seems natural to see Russell's notion of 'knowledge by acquaintance' as the heir of Plato's attempt to model Knowledge on vision . . . Plato and Russell think that unless this analogue to the forced character of visual perception occurs, there will be no distinction between knowledge and opinion, logic and mysticism, science and poetry . . .

Paull   There seems little doubt, then, that a great deal hangs on perception—and in particular, visual perception.

David   Luria's findings illustrate the variability that is possible in the kind of thinking that we all call perceiving. First of all, with respect to that old chestnut about seeing colours—investigation amongst the Uzbek showed that the use of categorical classifications depended on the kind of group being asked. The collective farm activists and young people with some formal education did not resist the sorting of wool or silk into groups of alike and not so alike (i.e. on the basis of hue). At the other extreme, the ichkari women, who were of course skilled with fabrics, could not be brought to classify according to a principle as abstract as colour:

> 'None of them are the same, you can't put them together . . .'
> 'This is like calf's dung, and this is like a peach . . .'

Often, when these subjects were pushed, they produced classifications which mixed colour with brightness or saturation. Luria goes on to claim: 'This unmediated way of relating to colours, without refracting them through the prism of categorical names, is very typical of this first group [i.e. women of the women's quarters] because their immediate practical experience abounds with such colour operations'.

Luria, p. 30

Paull The ichkari women were classifying according to a concrete or figurative principle—using their experience as a guide. But, I should add here that it was concrete and figurative from our point of view, at least.

David Yes, that is an important qualification—'from our point of view' the graphic and object names are particularising, not categorial: *lake*; *pig's dung*; *cotton in bloom*, etc.

The variability of perception is revealed more dramatically, however, as one turns to the work on the naming and classification of geometrical figures.

Paull Okay. You are now examining the universalist claims which arose with the European Gestalt psychologists . . .?

David Yes. Luria summarises their work helpfully: they 'tried to describe the basic laws of structural perception in order to find the processes that united psychology and physics and that constituted **the natural basis of human cognitive processes**'. I emphasise these last words of the quote in order to reiterate the issues previously mentioned—the argument between a conventional or a natural basis for our sense of reality.

Luria, p. 31

Paull Now, what was the method in the case of shapes?

David Relatively straightforward again. The subjects were asked to name shapes, and group and explain likenesses and contrasts. Here are examples of the figures. You can see how, from our point of view some are incomplete or merely suggested.

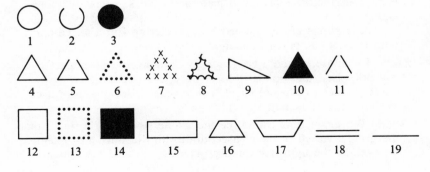

Figure 7
Geometrical figures presented to subjects

Luria, p. 33

45

Now the results paralleled what was found in the case of colours—the enquiries produced only the names of objects amongst the ichkari women; and these women did **not** envisage the figures as incomplete shapes (in the way Gestalt psychology would lead us to expect).

Luria points out that the results obtained in the original Gestalt experiments must be considered in the light of the highly-educated subjects. When the experience of the subjects is graphic-functional rather than rational, assumptions concerning perception need to be revised.

Here, for instance, are the responses of a nineteen-year-old ichkari woman

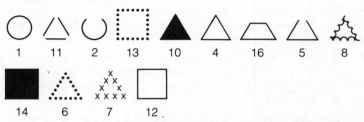

The subject defined 1 as a plate, 11 as a tent, 2 as a bracelet, 13 as beads, 10 as a tumar, 4 as a kettle-stand, 16 as a mirror, 5 as a cradle, 8 as a gold tumar, 14 as a mirror, 6 as an Uzbek clock, 7 as a silver tumar, and 12 as a mirror. When asked to classify the figures, she put 7 and 8 together ('they are valuable tumars'), and also 12, 14, and 16 ('mirrors'), declaring that none of the others were similar.

Luria, pp. 37—8

Paull So, rather than an answer based on qualities abstracted from all the objects of experience, this subject is offering only the concrete particulars of her habitual activities. In fact, the latter is what she sees! Is that the point of Luria's term graphic-functional?

David I think so. But there is more to recognising these differences between, say, the findings of the Gestalt psychologists and the responses in Uzbekistan. First of all, the variability suggests that visual perception involves more than any mechanism which is biologically inherited. And second, the differences suggest that whatever is involved in vision—at least, whatever is involved over and above the 'mechanism'—may undergo change in accordance with historical factors—in particular, factors relevant to patterns of work, social relations, and education.

These points are developed by considering Luria's findings with respect to optical illusions.

Paull I suppose it would be generally thought, even amongst psychologists, that optical illusions are in all cases the consequences of physiological 'constraints'. Illusions inform us of the limits of human vision.

David But again, this cannot be the whole story. Luria found that the groups varied in their susceptibility to illusions. For example on average the more educated groups experienced the optical

46

illusions (see 1—9) while the ichkari women and the peasants did not 'see' the illusions. Differences in this regard were particularly evident when the illusion involved geometrical shapes and perspective (e.g. 3 and 5). Only the Muller-Lyer illusion appeared effective across all groups (see illusion no. 6).

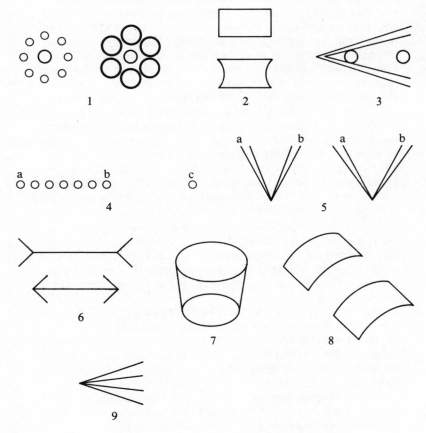

Figure 8
Optical illusions presented to subjects in different groups

Luria, p. 42

So, the researchers concluded that these findings were evidence of the role of social and historical conditions in seeing.

Paull Certainly, if there is such variability in perception—the 'bedrock' of cognitive processing—it would seem likely that greater variation will emerge as one studies problem-solving, reasoning, imagination, and ideas of the self.

David Yes. The differences between European cultural assumptions and the assumptions of the Uzbeks become more dramatic as we turn to Luria's work on reasoning and inference.

Paull Alright. But, just before we move to those findings, I would like to examine aspects of vision which you have not said enough about.

I'm worried about how much could be explained

Note the reference
to David Marr's
Vision in Israel
Rosenfield's article,
'Seeing through the
brain', *New York
Review*, Oct. 11,
1984, p. 53.

physiologically. David Marr's recent work, *Vision*, is a case in point. And we ought to reconsider Gregory's investigations. The study of the eye from an intra-organism perspective seems to suggest that there are specific strategies for resolving the information of the external world, and that these strategies are built into the very structure of the optical mechanism. For example, a frog will starve if you hang its food about it in a way that no movement occurs—its vision requires the movement in the object of sight. In a related way, human eyes resolve information according to certain selective programs. Changes in light intensity, according to Marr, are computed by the brain because the visual system has evolved on the basis that the changes are salient—they mark the edges and boundaries of objects in the world. Combined with this kind of situation is the possibility that particular neuronal networks have very specific functions—for instance, that some will interpret wide differences of intensity, and others will deal with fine differences. And ultimately, of course, one has to look at all this information going together, to its being integrated in such a way that a human being will not misinterpret a set of intensity differences: perhaps, by 'seeing' two objects where there is only one.

David Very well. Let's consider the idea of evolved structure in the system of vision. Marr refers to the assumptions built into this system as a set of constraints. This notion is part of a tradition of describing the brain. Essentially this tradition says that the organism has evolved such that it can perform task A but not task X.

Again, it seems to me that Popper has a concept which helps clarify this point. He regards the whole structure of the human organism as a veritable series of hypotheses concerning the nature of the external world. So, even the opposable thumb on the human hand has to be viewed as a kind of assumption, or constraint, on the form of experience.

In this respect, the facts which have been highlighted about the organisation of the eye are not different from other facts concerning physiological structure and information.

Paull Well, that only makes your case weaker, doesn't it?

David The point I am stressing is this: what matters is not the high degree of structure already in the information that the brain interprets; what matters is the scheme of things into which that information must fit. This information will have its own place in the activities of the organism—it will have a particular value (as we defined this term after Saussure).

As I see it, Luria's work emphasises the degree to which structural similarity can produce functional diversity.

Paull I see; again it is not the item that is important, but its place in a system.

David Well, yes. In this case the system is the pattern of cultural habits. This system has its own criteria of salience and its own purposes. One of the points stressed by Vygotsky and Luria is that changes in work, literacy, and formal education, create 'new motives for action'—new ends to which the organism is directed; and ultimately, new principles of organisation.

It is helpful to recall the observation mentioned earlier: namely, that a child thinks by remembering and an adult remembers by thinking. In what sense should one say the child and the adult are 'seeing' the world in the **same** way, through the **same** physiological mechanism? The process of seeing has to be considered in the context of the system of meanings within which the seeing fulfils a purpose.

Paull Now you must be using the words 'meaning' and 'purpose' in a broad, maybe over-general, way . . . I wonder how one could regard a newborn child's vision. Is it appropriate to talk about a system of meanings and purpose in the very young child?

David Again it is a situation of same and different. The experiments and theories of Trevarthen at Edinburgh, as well as of Newson and Bullowa, indicate the intensity of communication (or quasi-conversation) in the first months of life. The mother and child, as we discussed earlier, constitute a dyadic system. I cannot see any plausible reason to assume that the child's perceptions exist in a semantic vacuum. The contact with the mum has its own meanings, although they are of a very different order to the signs which constitute the words and grammar of a natural language. Besides the 'proto-conversations' which Trevarthen describes (through his split screen recordings of mother and child), Brazelton has found that it is important that the mum discern the drift of her baby's activities—she needs to let him taper off or to raise the level of action in accordance with natural cycles in the child. In the tight reciprocity between mother and baby, actions realise meanings. Clearly, we cannot talk about a system of arbitrary signs. Still, it would be equally wrong to think that the baby's perceptions are without a context of meaningful behaviours.

Paull What about 'purpose'?

David I think Trevarthen's work on primary and secondary 'inter-subjectivity' shows how the child participates in goal-oriented behaviour. In the former, the end or goal is the interaction itself; with the latter, the secondary, the child is working to bring some object (a 'topic'!) into the interaction.

Paull Overall, then, your view of the visual system stresses how data from the external world are integrated. Even for the newborn, inter-subjectivity brings its own criteria of salience.

David This situation—with interaction establishing values—also emphasises another point, I feel. In the same way that it made no sense to separate thought from signs, so too it seems to me that biological and cultural evolution are mutually defining. This can be expressed in another way: an intra-organism theory will ultimately require an inter-organism perspective, and vice versa.

See C. Trevarthen, 'Communication and co-operation in early infancy: a description of primary intersubjectivity', and J. Newson, 'The growth of shared understandings between infant and caregiver', in Margaret Bullowa (ed.), *Before Speech: The Beginning of Interpersonal Communication*, Cambridge University Press, Cambridge, 1979.

This, perhaps, sounds too grand a generalisation; but it is the kind of paradox we can place in a clearer light now that we have experienced the difficulties in Saussurean theory.

Paull   Yes. I can see that we have dealt with a number of instances of reciprocal definition. In such situations it is illegitimate to discuss either side of the definition as if it could be isolated. It reminds me of the various 'koan' or paradoxes of Zen Buddhism: e.g. the sound of one hand clapping, and so on.

David   Yes. And your mention of this teaching device-cum-riddle brings me back to the Uzbek and Luria's study.

Luria's team obtained some of their most dramatic results in their use of syllogisms. As mentioned before, syllogisms were presented to the subjects in the mode of traditional puzzles or riddles. The syllogisms were also of two distinct types—those that drew on what was familiar to the villagers, and those syllogisms which use unfamiliar content. The following conversation exemplifies the responses from those oriented to the graphic-functional modes of thinking:

Subject: Abdurakhm, age thirty-seven, from remote Kashgar village, illiterate.

Cotton can grow only where it is hot and dry. In England it cold and damp. Can cotton grow there?
'I don't know.'
Think about it.
'I've only been in the Kashgar country; I don't know beyond that . . .
[Refusal; reference to lack of personal experience.]
But on the basis of what I said to you, can cotton grow there?
'If the land is good, cotton will grow there, but if it is damp and poor, it won't grow. If it's like the Kashgar country, it will grow there too. If the soil is loose, it can grow there too, of course.'
[Both premises ignored, reasoning conducted within the framework of conditions advanced independently.]
The syllogism is repeated. What can you conclude from my words?
'If it's cold there, it won't grow; if the soil is loose and good, it will.'
[Conditions of syllogism ignored.]
But what do my words suggest?
'Well, we Moslems, we Kashgars, we're ignorant people; we've never been anywhere, so we don't know if it's hot or cold there'.
[The same.]
The following syllogism is presented: In the Far North, where there is snow, all bears are white. Novaya Zemlya is in the Far North and there is always snow there. What color are the bears there?
'There are different sorts of bears.'
[Failure to infer from syllogism.]
The syllogism is repeated.
'I don't know; I've seen a black bear, I've never seen any others . . .
Each locality has its own animals: if it's white, they will be white; if it's yellow, they will be yellow.'
[Appeals only to personal, graphic experience.]

50

But what kind of bears are there in Novaya Zemlya?

'We always speak only of what we see; we don't talk about what we haven't seen'.

[The same.]

But what do my words imply? The syllogism is repeated.

'Well, it's like this: our tsar isn't like yours, and yours isn't like ours. Your words can be answered only by someone who was there, and if a person wasn't there he can't say anything on the basis of your words.'

[The same.]

But on the basis of my words—in the North, where there is always snow, the bears are white, can you gather what kind of bears there are in Novaya Zemlya?

'If a man was sixty or eighty and had seen a white bear and had told about it, he could be believed, but I've never seen one and hence I can't say. That's my last word. Those who saw can tell, and those who didn't see can't say anything!' (At this point a young Uzbek volunteered, 'From your words it means that bears there are white'.)

Well, which of you is right?

'What the cock knows how to do, he does. What I know, I say, and nothing beyond that!'

Luria, pp. 108—9

Paull There are very many observations one might wish to make on that exchange. I mean, besides what Abdurakhm will **not** be drawn into, there are many positive features to his approach.

David I agree. We certainly don't have to make any excuses for the graphic-functional mode of thinking. It is unfortunate, however, that the whole investigation was not well received in Russia during the 1930s. It was mistakenly regarded as research which could be insulting to various national groups.

   Luria described the characteristics of the graphic-functional subjects:

   a 'a mistrust of initial premises that did not arise out of their personal experience.'
   b a failure 'to accept such premises as universal'.
   c a tendency to disintegrate the syllogism 'into three isolated, particular propositions with no unified logic'. . .

A. R. Luria, *The Making of Mind: A Personal Account of Soviet Psychology*, (ed.) Michael Cole & Sheila Cole, Harvard University Press, USA, 1979, p. 79

Paull Well, those three points appear to me somewhat negative in their wording. What strikes me about the answer is the degree to which they distinguish between actual and hypothetical knowledge. By 'actual' I mean something like, I suppose, 'knowledge by acquaintance'—knowledge based on reports of the senses. This distinction could be viewed from the Uzbek point of view; that is, as a feature, not as a limitation.

David Yes. I wonder what the Uzbek thought of many of the 'right' answers discussed in these experiments, since a number of the problems and syllogisms posed were designed with premises which all the participants knew to be incorrect: for example, that town X was closer than town Y. Of course, reasoning with a syllogism one doesn't ask about the truth of the premises so much as the validity of the logical inference. Separating truth from thinking must have appeared astonishing to Abdurakhm—like an alien form of sophistry. .

Paull I am intrigued also by the political and social consequences of the graphic-functional orientation. Would such a perspective make one less vulnerable to certain kinds of propaganda—all the hypothetical talk of a 'thousand year Reich', of 'Lebensraum', of fighting for 'democracy', and of a 'proletariat of the future'.

David I'm sure this is one area of observation Luria may not have felt free to address. But you have already mentioned the significance of Abdurakhm's replies: they constitute an alternative view of what meanings are salient. The distinction actual/hypothetical is not a semantic opposition around which the resources of Modern English are marshalled. My claim can be argued firstly by considering Modern English in relation to Middle English.

When Chaucer was writing *The Canterbury Tales* (around 1380) the English he used marked many kinds of hypothetical meanings explicitly. So the wide variety of ways we make projections about wishes, desires, hopes etc. could have been signalled by the selection of certain forms of the verb. The 'Yet-to-be-fulfilled' was encoded in the subjunctive mood. Now, for better or for worse, the use of the subjunctive is not a genuine option of Modern English: it occurs only in one or two almost frozen constructions such as 'If I *were* you . . .' rather than 'If I was you . . .'.

In a related way, a number of auxiliary verbs have lost some of their volitional significance. For instance, the auxiliary *will* seems to have more to do with futureness than the volition.

Now, I don't want to suggest that one can make simple correlations between single grammatical features and cultural perspective. One cannot. Connections between a linguistic system and patterns of culture have to be argued by showing how very many, apparently autonomous choices across the culture are congruent. Furthermore, one has to be able to display both explicit and implicit meanings. Hasan's 'Ways of Saying: Ways of Meaning' is one of very few studies which addresses these problems squarely. In Whorf's writings too, the major emphasis is on what he refers to as 'covert categories'. But more of that later.

The point that emerges from the opposition you mentioned (actual/hypothetical) is that communities can vary significantly with respect to their habit **and** resources for meaning,

Paull It has occurred to me how closely Abdurakhm's final words parallel the famous claim by the young Wittgenstein, when he was committed to the propositions of the *Tractatus*: 'what we cannot talk about we must pass over in silence'.

David Yes. This ironic parallel does bring out, albeit in a light-hearted way, the importance of cultural context—the 'positivism' of the Uzbek is a philosophy like any other. Even Luria seems to me a little too negative on this point.

R. Hasan, 'Ways of saying: Ways of meaning', in R. P. Fawcett (ed.) et. al., *The Semiotics of Culture and Language*, Volume 1, *Language as Social Semiotic*, Frances Pinter, London, 1984

L. Wittgenstein, *Tractatus Logico-Philosophicus*, Routledge & Kegan Paul, London, 1974, p. 3

Paull It is likely, in this regard, that the rational thinker is always going to interpret the graphic-functional as somewhat limited. There is a sense in which Abdurakhm **does** miss connections or relationships, don't you agree?

David I am not sure what is the significance of the limits **we** see in the responses to the syllogisms. It is important also to consider what Abdurakhm does that in our culture we don't!

Paull As you know, I am very receptive to the careful qualifications which you are seeking. But here, it might be argued that the Uzbek is not recognising certain relationships which are prior to any culture—they are conditions on the very nature of experience. Take the law of excluded middle, for example: something cannot be both 'a' and 'not a' at the same time. It is in this area of logical law, and also perhaps with respect to number, that one finds the most plausible claims concerning universals.

From numbers to *lingua mentalis*

David Oh, I concede that many aspects of reality have been regarded as 'a priori'. But how justified are we in using **our** sense of the world to argue for these universals? I can illustrate this point again using Yallop's discussion of 'Numerals in Australian Aboriginal Languages'. The analogy with inference amongst the Uzbek is direct.

Yallop begins from a point of wide agreement: namely, that Australian Aboriginal languages do not have highly developed resources for numbering and number operations. He further notes that linguists are both inconsistent and condescending in explaining away this fact. Most often they suggest that Aborigines had little need to count, that Aborigines were concerned with the concrete not the abstract, and that Aborigines **can** learn Western mathematics.

Behind these last claims there is the assumption that number is a universal: if a language does not have highly developed means of enumeration etc., then that 'deficiency', *vis-à-vis* European cultures, needs to be explained.

But as Yallop shows through textual comparisons, it could be similarly argued that Australian Aboriginal languages exhibit greater emphasis and development with respect to notions of duality (including two-ness; pairing; complementary relationships, and so on). Certainly, it seems beyond question that these languages have far greater grammatical resources for making duality explicit.

Having established this difference between European languages and Australian Aboriginal languages, Yallop then offers two crucial observations:

Michael Christie, *Aboriginal Perspectives on Experience and Learning: The Role of Language in Aboriginal Education*, (ECS806 Sociocultural aspects of language and education) Deakin University, Geelong, Vic., 1985

Yallop, 'Numerals in Australian Aboriginal languages', unpublished manuscript, p. 17

   i If Aborigines wanted to offer a defence of the importance of pairing and duality I think they might find reasons just as 'natural' and persuasive as our conviction that numerals are essential to manipulation of the world. They could appeal to the 'objective' duality of nature, the maleness and femaleness of humanity, the duality of the body with two eyes, ears, arms, breasts, etc., the opposition of night and day, sun and moon, winter and summer, and so on. They could argue that their own social structure, with moieties divided into sections and sections sometimes further divided into subsections, their camp layout with opposing sides forming the whole, the frequent reciprocity and cyclicity of their kinship terminology, that all of these aspects of human life merely reflect the natural state of affairs, where the fundamental duality of reality far outweighs the trivial matter of number.

Yallop, p. 18

ii If there is any validity in what I've been trying to explore, then there **is** a real gap between Western and Aboriginal culture. But it is not a gap between complexity and simplicity, civilisation and primitiveness, nor even between the mathematically precise and the concretely naïve, but rather between two different **kinds** of complexity and civilisation and abstraction.

In my view Yallop's discussion is primarily a warning. It is a warning against neutralising the significant difference which may occur between cultures. In particular, it is a warning against using products of **our** cultural development as a means of calibrating achievements in other cultures. The danger arises when we regard certain kinds of meaning as supra-historical.

It is interesting to note, for example, that even the law of the excluded middle is not unshakable. Heisenberg has given particular emphasis to the limitations of this axiom when describing subatomic phenomena. In other words, there is even a boundary condition within our own culture to which this basic logical axiom cannot be extended.

Paull If 'logical laws' and 'numerals' are not quite the plausible universals I had thought, perhaps, we should consider language structures themselves as candidates for universality. I'm aware that there has been a great deal of attention given to language universals. And I note that Chomsky states universals have been established 'empirically'. How might language universals bear on our comparison between the Uzbek and Modern European cultures?

David Yes, as diffuse as this topic is, it is important to confront claims concerning linguistic universals. I would just mention first, however, that I questioned the universal or a priori character of logical laws and numerals specifically because logic and number could be regarded as products of the culture, just like any other subsystem across the meaning potential of a given culture. There seems to me no reason to think that these meanings are the only legitimate and natural way to develop, just as I do not think that Western art has to evolve in accordance with aesthetic principles traditional to Japan.

But now, some comment on the question of language universals . . . From the perspective of someone outside linguistics this debate can appear extremely confusing. For that reason I will divide the topic into five uses of the word universal. This division does not exhaust the topic, it merely separates the aspects most relevant to our present themes. Universals have been suggested with respect to:

1 the form of coding systems;
2 the forms of actual human languages (i.e. natural languages);
3 the possible forms of a human language;
4 the basic meanings which constitute a *lingua mentalis* (i.e. a language of mind);
5 the general functions of human language.

While these five divisions obviously interrelate, it is also crucial to be able to distinguish between them, as they have quite distinct implications for the description of language. Under point (1) we might consider a range of issues, including the linearity of messages, the discreteness of messages, the role of redundancy, and the 'open' character of the possible messages produced by the system. These very general matters needn't take up our attention, except in one case.

It is important to realise that human languages are extremely economical in the way that they can be used to encode such a wide range of meanings through such small sets of constituent elements. Looked at rather schematically, we can say that meanings (semantics) are encoded in words and syntax (lexico-grammar) which is in its turn encoded in a set of sounds (phonology). This tri-stratal organisation is fundamental to the character of human languages (i.e. in contrast with animal languages). And, as was mentioned in the previous discussion, it is the main principle which distinguishes an adult system of speech from the proto-linguistic system of the child's earliest communications—a system which makes use of only two levels.

Point (2) refers to the various claims that have been made concerning particular phonological, grammatical, and semantic categories. I'm sorry that my treatment of these claims may seem a little perfunctory. It is not that the claims are uninteresting in themselves. On the contrary. But two matters limit their importance in a discussion of talking and thinking. The first of these is general.

Statements of universals depend on the use of a common apparatus of linguistic description. This results in a vagueness about the universals—it is difficult to know how much is obscured and how much is imposed by the terms of the description. To illustrate this, I would simply ask you to think back to Saussure's ideas (from the 'point of view' determining the object, to the concept of value). Now with those ideas in mind reflect on the following universals suggested by Charles F.Hockett:

4.8: A major form-class distinction reminiscent of 'noun' versus 'verb' is universal, though not always at the same size-level.

4.9: Even human language has a common clause type with bipartite structure in which the constituents can reasonably be termed 'topic' and 'comment'.

Charles F. Hockett, 'The problem of universals in language', in Joseph H. Greenberg (ed.), *Universals of Language*, MIT Press, London, 1966, pp. 1-30

4.10: Every language has a distinction between one-referent ['Mary is singing'] and two-referent predicators ['John struck Bill'].

Note that 'noun' and 'verb' are class terms of the classical Western tradition. 'Topic' and 'comment' are ill-defined notions which approximate the narrower classical distinction 'subject and predicate'. Hockett's use of one and two referent predicators entails further aspects of the Western philosophical system—it is interesting, for example, that processes, events, or actions cannot be 'referents' in the terminology under discussion.

The other matter which leads us away from the forms of actual languages is simply that Chomsky's idea of a universal grammar is more abstract; and it is Chomsky's theory which precipitated most of the contemporary debate. Although he makes reference to the 'empirical' studies (which he sees as supporting his own work), Chomsky's universalism comes under point (3): 'the **possible** forms of a human language'. Chomsky has emphasised 'formal invariants of language'. These are general principles which apply to the 'formal operations that modify the form of sentences as well as rules of interpretation of sentences.'

Noam Chomsky, *Problems of Knowledge and Freedom*, Fontana Collins, Great Britain, 1972, p. 38

Chomsky's aim was to isolate those principles of language which **cannot** be explained on functional grounds, and which can therefore be considered **non-essential** to the operation of a coding system. According to his theory, such deep, abstract principles would be a 'mirror of the mind' in the sense that they would display the conditions and forms of organisation demanded by the structure of the brain. You can see that this approach is seeking the 'properties' of a human language faculty. This faculty Chomsky interprets as a species-specific 'mental organ'.

Paull   And this is why Chomsky's views stress the 'innate' and the 'a priori'?

David   Yes. Languages, in a sense, must be organised around certain principles—namely, the principles which constitute the basic, pre-conditions of thought.

Paull   But this claim appears both more general and more vague than the hypothesis that the human brain is wired with a grammar, a kind of core from which actual languages have been elaborated.

David   Well, the task of clarifying a universal grammar has always been, for Chomsky, one facet of cognitive psychology. His view of psychology has grown out of rationalist theories of the mind.

Accordingly one can have great difficulty in pinning down what would falsify Chomsky's theories. This is to say, the hypotheses appear to shift ground: while thought and language are very different in the theory, the organisation of language and the principles of thought are merged in debates. I take this to be the force of your last comment: as the 'principles' become more abstract and more general, it makes less sense to propose a universal grammar and a specific language faculty.

The fuzzy edges of the hypotheses can be seen, for instance, in the following summary presented by Chomsky in 1975.

Chomsky, *Reflections*, p. 43

> The place of the language faculty within cognitive capacity is a matter for discovery, not stipulation. The same is true of the place of grammar within the system of acquired cognitive structures. My own, quite tentative, belief is that there is an autonomous system of formal grammar, determined in principle by the language faculty and its component UG. This formal grammar generates abstract structures that are associated with 'logical forms' (in a sense of this term to which I will return) by further principles of grammar. But beyond this, it may well be impossible to distinguish sharply between linguistic and non-linguistic components of knowledge and belief. Thus an actual language may result only from the interaction of several mental faculties, one being the faculty of language. There may be no concrete specimens of which we can say, These are solely the product of the language faculty; and no specific acts that result solely from the exercise of linguistic functions.

Paull I can see why you feel there is a problem here with respect to 'falsification' : what does Chomsky count as evidence of a specific language faculty?

David Let's look at two kinds of argument—one related to language development in children, and the other to formal invariants (or universals).

With respect to young children, it was claimed by researchers within Chomsky's transformational-generative paradigm that children 'mastered' a system for generating an infinite variety of sentences in a very short time and on the basis of limited and 'degenerate' data (i.e. the talk that children actually hear between the ages of two and four). So the theory went. Investigations of what children actually hear and actually communicate, even before the age of two, force a total review of Chomsky's approach. His idea of a 'language acquisition device' has lost its *raison d'être*, since it was postulated to bridge the supposed gap between what a child knew and the child's linguistic experience. Furthermore, the ideas of children 'mastering' the language by the age of four, and of language as an infinity of sentences . . . well . . . these also illustrate academic myopia. There is just so much more to language than the sentence structures in evidence at kindergarten!

See again Clare Painter, *Learning the Mother Tongue*.

Paull From what you say, the plausibility of Chomsky's theory will depend greatly on his own examples of universals.

David In order to address this topic within manageable limits, I can report to you a point especially emphasised by Chomsky.

He stresses that all languages make use of 'structure dependent operations' and not 'structure independent' ones. In terms of the Saussurean theory we have discussed, the operations of language apply to the different elements arranged

Chomsky, *Problems of Knowledge and Freedom*, pp. 29—31

into a syntagm. One way to ask a question in English, for example, is to move the finite element of the clause in front of the element which functions as subject. In this way, 'The school pupils will be attending the carnival' can be made into the related structure '**Will** [the school pupils] be attending the carnival?'

Paull   So a 'structure dependent operation' depends on my being able to recognise the elements of the syntagm . . . That is, I have to be able to identify finite and subject and so on . . .?

David   Yes. On the other hand, if the rules had been independent of structure, they might be 'Take the left most element', or 'Take the fourth element' etc.

Paull   That is, rules that do not depend on the recognition of grammatical functions or elements . . .?

Chomsky, *Problems of Knowledge and freedom*, p. 30

David   Yes. Chomsky claims it is a surprising fact that human languages are structure dependent since, he feels, there is greater simplicity in structure independence.

Paull   So, according to Chomsky, there is no functional reason for the structure dependence . . .?

David   And since there is no functional explanation, Chomsky concludes that the structure dependence must mirror the special properties of the human mind.

Paull   Oh, okay; in this way one can make inferences about the mind on the basis of linguistic universals.

Chomsky, *Problems of Knowledge and Freedom*, p. 30

David   Chomsky sees structure dependence as part then of the 'innate schematism applied by the mind to the data of experience'.

I think there are a number of problems in Chomsky's claims concerning structure dependence, and I will mention one of these before moving on to the fourth kind of universalism cited in our five-point list.

There are no compelling reasons to accept that structure **in**dependent rules are more simple and therefore more functional. Structure dependence results in an enormous increase in the communicative potential of a message. This is because the place of an item (*vis-à-vis* all the other items) is itself significant. As we know from our Saussurean theory, the various grammatical relations are 'signs' just like words and other meaningful oppositions in a language.

In essence, structure dependence is an economical way of enriching the possible contrasts—the relations—which are the basis of a semiotic system. Chomsky's idea of 'structure independence' seems to imply that language could be organised as a simple aggregate of moves and bits; but what a gargantuan, unwieldy kind of aggregation that would be, at least by comparison with our present languages. On balance, it seems to me that structure dependence has just the kind of a functional explanation Chomsky eschews.

Other, smaller, difficulties could be mentioned also. How is it, for instance, that the structure independent decoder would isolate units from the phonological continuity of speech? And, in a structure independent system of signs, would all the signs be merely signifiers (in the Saussurean sense of this term)?

Paull One point I would like to mention here relates to the idea of an innate language faculty. It seems to me quite plausible that in the evolution of man some selection for language ability has occurred. If you concede that communication is important, then it follows that there would be selection for whatever abilities are fundamental to communicating. Don't you agree?

David In fact, Chomsky quotes the biologist Jacques Monod precisely on this queston. In *Chance and Necessity*, Monod suggests that linguistic capacity may now be 'a part of "human nature"', itself intimately associated with other aspects of cognitive function which may in fact have evolved in a specific way by virtue of the early use of articulated language'.

Jacques Monod,
*Chance and
Necessity*, Collins,
Fontana Books,
Glasgow, 1974,
pp. 151−2

This, of course, sounds plausible; and it brings out an interdependence between cultural and biological evolution. Still, what status has a universal grammar in this approach?

From our discussion of Saussure, we can see that the basis of language is the notion of contrast or opposition. We also discussed the two major types of these contrasts. First of all there are the contrasts which operate *in absentia*—the contrasts with all the options which might have been selected but were not. These are the paradigmatic relations.

The second type are those contrasts which operate *in praesentia*—the contrasts with all the other elements which are present in a particular configuration. These constitute the syntagmatic relations.

A third factor should be mentioned, but it is actually implicit in the above. This is the interrelation between paradigm and syntagm.

Now for my answer to your question about evolution and innateness . . . My answer arises out of the Saussurean theory of relations of relations of relations, and out of the distinction between the paradigmatic and the syntagmatic. If these kinds of oppositon or contrast are at the centre of the language system, then it follows that they would constitute the only necessary condition for the development of language.

Paull I think I see what you are suggesting: a facility for operating with these kinds of relations could be subject to natural selection. Hence, there would be no reason to postulate a separate, autonomous, language faculty. Is that where your argument is leading?

David Yes, as long as we add some comment on how this speculation differs from the notion of a universal grammar. The principles of organisation which I have focused on are relevant to the analysis of phenomena of very many kinds—not merely grammatical, symbolic, or semiotic systems. This is in part indicated by the way Saussure illustrates the terms value and paradigmatic/syntagmatic: the analogies with money and architecture, respectively.

In other words, the principles are of a very general and abstract kind. They can be interpreted, I believe, as ways of establishing firstly differences, and secondly similarities amidst differences. This sounds paradoxical, no doubt. But it is a paradox that recurs across disciplines as far apart as physics and literary analysis. The human organism puts differences, and similarities amidst differences, to many uses. Bateson, for example, describes perception as 'news of difference'. And this can be illustrated in the way binocular vision (two different views) creates our perception of depth.

While all of these considerations must be envisaged within the context of a theory of evolution, there seems to me no gain in postulating a specific language faculty and a universal grammar. Richard Gregory, for example, questions Chomsky's theories of innateness: 'What seems far more likely is that the deep structure of language has somehow developed from the much earlier perceptual structures of the object-hypotheses inherent in perception. Perhaps the invention of symbols was sufficient for this to take place—to externalise the structure of perception in language.'

See David Bohm, *Wholeness and the Implicate order*, Routledge & Kegan Paul, London, 1980, and Bateson, *Mind and Nature*. On relationships in literature see Chapter 1, 'Refractions: Interpretation through structural analysis' in L. Michael O'Toole, *Structure, Style and Interpretation in the Russian Short Story*, Yale University Press, London, 1982.

Gregory, p. 165

Paull I would think your argument can also be illustrated by reflecting on the 'hierarchical' organisation of living systems. There are many reasons why a hierarchical structure is functional—in particular, it facilitates adaptation. From what you have said about the strata of language—the levels of meaning, of lexico-grammar, and of phonology—hierarchical organisation is basic to language. Certainly though, one doesn't need a language specific faculty to explain it.

David Well, don't forget Chomsky was seeking those factors which could **not** be explained by function. But I still think your point is a good one. One cannot conceive of structure dependence in language without the concept of hierarchy: within the level of grammar there is a rank scale of structures (clause-complex/sentence; clause; group; word; morpheme . . .). So hierarchy is essential to one of Chomsky's central claims.

It might be appropriate now to consider the last two ideas on universal aspects of language, and then to move back to the research of Vygotsky and Luria.

Point (4) on universals referred to a *lingua mentalis*—a language of the mind. These words are, in fact, the title of a study by Anna Wierzbicka. By contrast with Chomsky's theory, Wierzbicka is ultimately concerned with semantic universals, not with formal invariants of syntax. Unlike Chomsky also, she is direct about what does or does not constitute a universal (or semantic prime). Furthermore, Wierzbicka's methodology is empirical and non-formalistic: 'elementary units of thought can

Anna Wierzbicka, *Lingua mentalis: The Semantics of natural language*, Academic Press, Sydney, 1980, p. 7

be reached only through paraphrases in natural language', not by analysis in terms of artificial symbols that are not self-explanatory.

Paull Is Wierzbicka's theory related to other theories, or in some ways out by itself?

David Wierzbicka sees her work in the context of a long, Western, philosophical tradition. From classical Greek philosophy, through St. Augustine, to Liebniz there has been, she argues, a search for a *lingua mentalis*—something totally distinct from interiorised natural language. Unlike Liebniz though, Wierzbicka actually offers the following list of thirteen items as the 'irreducible core' of all languages. This is to say, the meanings of any language can be paraphrased without calling on any meanings outside of these 'semantic primitives':

I	someone	world	want	think of	be part of
you	something	this	not want	say	become
				imagine	

For Wierzbicka these meanings constitute what Liebniz called 'the alphabet of human thought'. To arrive at these, Wierzbicka did not draw on intuition (a method much used in Chomskyan linguistics). Rather she tested the possibility of stating one notion in terms of another. The meanings above are those which resisted reduction **into terms which were themselves more basic**. For example *change* was found to be more basic than *motion* since all motions involve change, but not all changes involve motion.

Wierzbicka, p. 4

Paull So the reduction is a form of the atomism we discussed in the preceding talk. . .?

David Definitely; though Wierzbicka's approach involves specific hypotheses and, as you can see, a method which constrains the arbitrary invention of universals.

Paull It seems to me, however, that this notion of semantic primes runs very much counter to the Saussurean approach to meaning and signs. It doesn't appear to rely at all on Malinowski either; that is, the thirteen meanings do not depend on actions in specific contexts.

David Perhaps I could offer just a few comments here before moving on to point (5) and then return to Luria in Uzbekistan. Wierzbicka's approach depends on being able to relate aspects of different languages, on being able to translate. Now in this procedure Wierzbicka must, of necessity, deal with the Saussurean concept of value. One cannot equate or relate terms across two systems simply by comparing significations. This is the problem we need to keep in focus when we are using natural language to describe a natural language. Wierzbicka mentions the problem obliquely through the words 'range of application'. But in the end she argues for the separation of 'meaning and range of application'. I find it difficult, then, to relate the

Wierzbicka, p. 27

concepts of sign and value to Wierzbicka's approach. What is, in fact, a sign? If thirteen meanings are prior to language, do all other signs emerge through aggregation?

On a more technical point—though again using our Saussurean background—the paraphrase method has to make use of syntagmatic relations, not just paradigmatic choices. This is obvious, I know. But it seems to me that not all the syntagmatic relations used in the paraphrases have been explicated by the thirteen terms.

So with respect to value above, we can see that the status of translation is vague. And with respect to syntagm, the method of paraphrase needs further development.

Paull   Yet translation and paraphrase are fundamental to any project of semantic reduction.

Halliday & Hasan, *Language, Context and Text,* and M. A. K. Halliday, *Spoken and Written Language*, Oxford University Press, Oxford, 1989.

David   Yes . . . The fifth use of universal relates to function rather than to either syntax or semantic primes. Halliday's theory of language has already been presented through a number of volumes in these two series on 'Language and Learning'. I will proceed, therefore, on the basis that the global character of the approach has been already understood.

In Halliday's interpretation, human language has evolved to fulfil three general functions—three 'meta-functions'. Accordingly the analysis of a text reveals three simultaneous strands of structure, unfolding through speech: an interpersonal strand, an ideational strand, and a textual strand. If we take a clause of English and examine the various ways in which that clause can be systematically varied, one can start to appreciate the many systems of choice which operate in a language. There are, for example, 'choices' of mood, transitivity, modality, tense, thematisation, informational focus, etc. as well as choices of words. In short, there are many kinds of choices at each of the grammatical ranks (mentioned above).

Paull   Maybe. But how is this any different from the claims of other contemporary theories of grammar?

David   Yes, well, just as the choices open to a speaker can be seen as relatively autonomous sets of options (i.e. systems), so too the different systems themselves fall together into three major blocks.

Paull   Why is it, though, that certain systems are closer together? What's the basis of the 'three blocks'?

David   The short answer is relatedness of function. And relatedness of function could be expressed as similarity of meaning. For example, the system of mood in English involves the following broad choices:

Figure 9

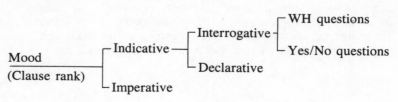

Another system that applies to clauses of English is modality. The options in this case cannot be so easily presented in a suitably small diagram. Modality involves, however, the gradations of certainty between an absolute *yes* and an absolute *no*. So the realisations of modality can be *possibly*, *probably*, *it is possible*, etc; or a choice based on the verbal group — *maybe. . ., could, might. . .* and so on. The system actually extends out to 'frequency of occurrence' on the one hand, and to 'necessity of occurrence' on the other.

Paull   Now your argument is, I imagine, that mood and modality exhibit relatedness of function . . .?

David   Yes. That is, similarity of meaning.

Paull   But the similarity is not transparent, is it?

David   Again, if you consider the systems in relation to other systems of choice the functional similarity is apparent. Halliday notes, however, that we are dealing with an abstract concept of function here—it is **not** simply another way of saying 'use'.

Both mood and modality contribute to the interpersonal meta-function: the systems offer the speaker various resources for organising his position in relation to other people. This is clear with respect to mood, since mood presents us with the forms by which requests, offers, orders, statements, etc. can be realised. What modality permits you to do, however, is to present points of view, and to mark these as personal, impersonal, etc.

The interpersonal function is particularly evident across these systems when one thinks of them in relation to transitivity. Transitivity is an ideational system at the rank of clause by which the speaker can describe the phenomena of experience. By comparison with transitivity, mood and modality are interactional in orientation: they are the means by which speakers can define roles, set-up and argue opposing opinions, and intervene in social activities.

Paull   Let me just check through and gloss the three meta-functions. Other than the interpersonal, which you have elaborated, there are the ideational and textual functions. Now the ideational meanings are those related to representing phenomena and states of affairs. The textual function of language . . . that is not so easy for me to envisage. How should one describe the textual function?

David   The textual function refers to those resources in the language by which discourse can be made to cohere with (a) other segments of discourse; and (b) the context of situation. The details of this function are, of course, handled in *Language, Context and Text* by Halliday and Hasan.

Paull   So Halliday's use of universal applies only to this idea that language will have means of expressing—you say 'realising'—the three meta-functions. Halliday is not offering us any universals in the structures of a language or, for that matter, in the structure of the organism which produces the language. Is that a fair account of the position?

David   With regard to 'structure' the functional approach creates something of a paradox. By considering discourse from the point of view of function, the analysis of structure is actually taken further than in models which purport to concentrate on structure alone. The functional interpretation highlights options which other models overlook, for example, thematisation and information focus.

Whereas Halliday's analysis treats text as a form of functional polyphony—with three patterns of choice combined into one line of linguistic form—other, non-functional, approaches tend to blur the choices open to a speaker. The blurring results in an appearance of greater randomness in linguistic variation. The analysis of a clause needs to keep together all those variations relevant to 'subject-ness' as against those relevant to 'actor-ness' or 'theme-ness'. So, ultimately, function gives a richer and more coherent view of structure. By comparison, Chomsky's approach again seems very limited: 'If language is to be thought of on the analogy of a physical organ such as the heart, then functional explanations are unlikely to carry us very far, and we should concern ourselves with the structure of the organ that serves these functions.'

Chomsky, *Reflections*, p. 59

But I have actually diverged from your summary of Halliday's position. Yes, I think your account is fair. We need only emphasise that, of the five uses of 'universal' which we have discussed, Halliday's use is unique in being oriented to society rather than to the organism.

Self: cogito ergo . . .? . ·. sumus?

Paull   Well, how do we take all this back to Uzbekistan, to Abdurakhm and the syllogisms in Luria's research?

David   It would be helpful to know more about the total system of which Abdurakhm's responses are a reflection. It is too easy to assume that the graphic-functional can only fulfil itself by passing on to the rational. As is suggested by Yallop's discussion of duality, there may be many ways in which a coherent model of phenomena can be constructed and justified.

For this reason, claims about universals can appear very ambivalent. Certain universals have arisen because we can't think of a given situation in any way but one.

Paull   Yes. You are implying that the universal could mark a fundamental limit on human thinking, or merely a limitation of particular minds at a particular point in cultural evolution.

David   The law of the excluded middle might be a case in point. On the one hand, it seems inconceivable that the descriptions 'a' and 'not a' could be simultaneously relevant. But, if Heisenberg is right, it may be that such tenets of rationalism cannot be extended to certain domains of phenomena.

Paull   I think that many people in our community live each day
with contradictions of the law of excluded middle: for example,
with respect to making 'free' decisions. I am aware that my
situation in the world—the options I have, the opinions I hold,
the assumptions I make—are determined by social and historical
forces. In this sense one might say the Marxists are right. Then
again, I am also aware of a kind of unlimited discretion: at any
point, I can decide for or against any course of action (as long
as, of course, I am willing to accept the consequences of my
actions). In this sense Camus, Sartre, and the Existentialists, are
right.

David   So you are suggesting that moral, and other, decisions can
involve this kind of contradiction. Well, I can recall a
theologian, Paul Tillich, proposing a similar interpretation of
free-will—that objectively one is committed to determinism
(causality, etc.), but from a subjective point of view one is a
free agent.

There are at least two comments that need to be considered:

First of all, as your example suggests, there may be
important areas of human experience in which an individual has
to handle something like a contradiction of the law of excluded
middle. It is not just that a phenomenon can have more than one
value (multivalence), it is that these values lead to opposed or
seemingly irreconcilable interpretations. For instance, despite
what Heisenberg has argued from physics, we operate on the
assumption that all events and states have causal explanations—at
least, in principle. This principle is set aside in a court of law,
however, in the act of punishing offenders: punishment only
makes sense when you believe that someone can cause a chain of
events without being equally the product of one.

It is important to note here that individuals vary in their
relationships to contradiction and multiple interpretations. Each
community varies also with respect to what might be called
'multiple ways of seeing'—the ways in which it integrates
competing interpretations of experience.

Michael Christie,
*Aboriginal
Perspectives*

Now I want to argue, in our next discussion, that this claim
brings us to one of the primary and most general functions of
education: namely, establishing multiple ways of seeing. My aim
is to concentrate on the role of language in establishing these
ways.

My second comment on your example brings us back to Luria
and Uzbekistan. Note that your idea of an individual with
unlimited discretion (your 'existentialist') actually depends on a
particular understanding of the 'self'. This would correspond to
what Luria calls the Cartesian view of self: namely, that 'self-
consciousness' is primary, with a 'secondary rank accorded to
the perception of the external world and other people'.

Luria, *Cognitive
Development*, p. 19

Vygotsky and Luria set out to observe the manifestations of
self-awareness amongst the five groups studied for perception

and reasoning. Their findings again varied in a consistent way across their groups. Overall, the groups with least contact with experiences beyond their local work tended to misconstrue all kinds of enquiry which related to an individualised, 'ideal self'. Questions concerning their own shortcomings, their aspirations, and their qualities (*vis-à-vis* other villagers) were answered according to a pattern. The peasants understood these enquiries only in terms of external circumstances—poverty, debt, dress—or in terms of overt behaviour—in particular, forms of talking. When some feature of character was mentioned, it typically arose in the description of others, and again related to manifested behaviour: e.g. *Akram is quick to get angry*.

The following excerpts illustrate the enquiries with peasants. Of special interest, it seems to me, is the way one subject (Murza Shiral) emphasises a direct relationship between the protocol of his talk and being *good-natured*. Hence, the character of *I* is typically established by a description of action with respect to others.

Luria, *Cognitive Development*, pp. 148–50

Subject: Karambai Khamb, age thirty-six, peasant from village of Yardan, illiterate.

Well, now, take yourself, Karambai, and your guest here, Ismat. What is the difference between you?

'There's no difference at all. Once there's a soul it means we're the same.'

What shortcomings and good qualities do you have? What's your character like? You know what character is?

'Yes!'

People can be good or bad, hot-tempered or calm. What sort of person are you?

'What can I say about my own heart?'

But who could tell about your heart other than you yourself?

'How can I talk about my character? Ask others; they can tell you about me. I myself can't say anything.'

[Reference to the fact that others can judge a man's character.]

What would you like to change or improve in yourself?

'I was a farmhand; I have a hard time and many debts, with a measure of wheat costing eighteen rubles—that's what troubles me'.

Well, people are different, and have different characters; what are you like?

'If I have a lot of money, I buy things and then I'm happy; if I don't have things I'm sad'.

[Derives own situation from the circumstances.]

Well, have you friends here in Yardan. Describe their character.

'There's Akram, and there's Ismat. They're different, of course. How can you know another's heart? One doesn't talk like the other . . . They're both good-natured . . . except that Akram is quick to get angry, but not Ismat.'

[Evaluation of others much more complete.]

66

Subject: Murza Shiral, age fifty-five, peasant from village of
Yardan, illiterate.

Do you think that people are all the same or different?
'No, they're not the same. There are different ones [holds up
fingers]: here's a landowner, here's a farmhand.'
Do you know what the differences are between individuals, say,
between your acquaintances?
'Only they themselves know?
Well, what are you like? Describe your character.
'My character is very good-natured. Even if it's a youngster who's
before me, I use the polite form of address and speak courteously
. . . You have to understand everything, and I don't.'
[Description of own behaviour.]
Still, do you have any shortcomings?
'I have many shortcomings, food, clothing, everything.'
Well, there are other people here in the village; are you the same
as them or not?
'They have their own hearts and different conversations, and they
speak different words.'
Well, compare yourself to them and describe your character.
'I'm a good-natured person, I talk to big people like a big person,
to little people like a little person, and to middle-sized people like a
middle-sized person . . . That's all I can say, there's nothing else
that remains.'
[The same.]

Paull This is what you meant then by the anti-Cartesian aspect of
a social interpretation of signs?

David Yes. One's private self ultimately depends on the system of
talk going on in the community. In this way the *Cogito ergo sum*
of Déscartes needs to be modified; perhaps *Cogito ergo sumus*:
'I think therefore we are'. But this doesn't do justice to the
relationship either.

Paull This is central to many issues in psychology and
philosophy, isn't it? For instance, the problem of being sure of a
world beyond my own private states and feelings. . . the
problem of solipsism. . . This problem can never arise when one
identifies the source of private thoughts in public speech.

David No, it doesn't, I agree. This was Wittgenstein's view, as I
understand it.

Paull Maybe we ought to consider counter-proposals at this stage.
What comment would you make about the following statement
by Herbert Feigl? He appears to be carrying the argument
beyond the inter-subjectivity of language and community
behaviour:

> As I see it, Wittgenstein's casuistic treatment of the problem is
> merely one of the more recent in a long line of positivistic
> (ametaphysical, if not anti-metaphysical) attempts to show that the
> mind-body problem arises out of conceptual confusions, and that
> proper attention to the way in which we use mental and physical

Herbert Feigl,
'Mind-Body, *Not* a
Pseudoproblem', in
S. Hook (ed.),
*Dimensions of
Mind*, Collier
Books, London,
1961, pp. 33—4

terms in ordinary language will relieve us of the vexatious problem. Gilbert Ryle, B.F. Skinner, and, anticipating all of them, R. Carnap, have tried to obviate the problem in a similar way: The use of mental or 'subjective' terms is acquired by learning the language we all speak in everyday life; this language, serving as a medium of communication among human beings, is by its very nature *inter-subjective*; it is on the basis of publicly accessible cues that, for example, the mother tells the child 'you feel tired,' 'now you are glad,' 'you have a headache,' etc., and that the child learns to use such phrases as 'feeling tired,' 'being glad,' 'having a headache,' as applied not only to others, but also to himself when he is in the sort of condition which originally manifested itself in the cues (symptoms, behaviour situations and sequences, test conditions and results, etc.) observable by others. But here is the rub. Even if we *learn* the use of subjective terms in the way indicated, once we have them in our vocabulary we *apply* them to states or conditions to which we, as individual subjects, have a 'privileged access'. If I report moods, feelings, emotions, sentiments, thoughts, images, dreams, etc., that I experience, I am *not referring to my behaviour*, be it actually occurring or likely to occur under specified conditions. I am referring to those states or processes of my direct experience which I live through (enjoy or suffer), to the 'raw feels' of my awareness. These 'raw feels' are accessible to other persons only indirectly by inference—but it is *myself* who *has* them.

David   This is a very useful summary, I think. Most particularly, however, because of its final error. Saussurean theory has been significant to our themes because, among other things, it has very specific implications for the relation between thought and language. The theory excludes the whole possibility of 'raw feels'—at least, with respect to our applications of 'subjective' terms and self-'awareness'. Remember the reciprocal nature of the *signifié* and *signifiant*. Isn't this Wittgenstein's point also? It makes no sense to talk about subjective terms (publicly acquired) and then go on to discuss raw feels. Feigl understands the answer but not the problem! His whole point concerning privileged access is hard to judge since it relies on a number of subjectivist terms—the terms which Wittgenstein worked to eliminate: who is this I/myself? And in what sense does it **have** raw feels?

Paull   Well, I imagine that there are other ways to this understanding of inter-subjectivity. One doesn't need to have come via Saussure, or Wittgenstein, surely?

David   On the particular question of the 'self' there are many interesting sources of comparable insights—that is, comparable to the findings of Luria in Uzbekistan.

For example, in discussing 'Homer's view of man', Bruno Snell claims that 'the belief in the existence of a universal, uniform human mind is a rationalist prejudice'. Snell finds in the language and literature of the Homeric period a set of terms for what we call 'mind'. But the Homeric terms—*thymos*, *noos*, and *psyche*—do not refer to subjective experience as such. Snell argues in detail that these terms have to be understood 'by the

Bruno Snell, *The Discovery of the Mind: The Greek origins of European thought*, (tr.) T. G. Rosenmeyer, Harper Torchbooks, New York, 1960, p. 16

analogy of physical organs'. Yet he notes that it is contradictory to use the term 'organ' in relation to the 'soul', or private experiences of 'will'.

Our transcription of 'psyche', 'noos' and 'thymos' as 'organs' of life, of perception, and of (e)motion are, therefore, merely in the nature of abbreviations, neither totally accurate nor exhaustive; this could not be otherwise, owing to the circumstance that the concept of the 'soul'—and also of the 'body', as we have seen—is tied up with the whole character and orientation of a language. This means that in the various languages we are sure to find the most divergent interpretations of these ideas. Snell, p. 15

Paull So he is suggesting that the subjective experience implicit in Homer's writing differs from our own?

David Yes. . .specifically in its subjectiveness. What Snell refers to as the *Discovery of the Mind* is the evolution of the notion of a private soul, with its attendant responsibilities and forms of awareness. Men leave behind a consciousness based on the organs of perception and emotion, etc. They also move away from a mind subject to the intervention of gods.

Paull In so much as Snell is stressing the role of language in revealing these different stages in the development of consciousness, it appears that we are again dealing with a semantic theory of the mind.

David Oh, yes. Very much so. Snell's work is relevant to Vygotsky's 'system-semantic' view of the mind. For instance, in his chapter on the origins of scientific thought, Snell stresses the role of meanings in creating the possibility of a scientific perspective. Hence, definiteness (i.e., the definite article) in Greek was crucial to the potential for certain kinds of generic and universalist statements. This, Snell argues, creates the further possibility of the abstractions of science. A simple example compares τὸ ἀγαθόν (the good) in Greek with Cicero's awkward translation: *id quod (re vera) bonum est* (perhaps: 'that which is good—true things'). Snell, p. 228

Paull You are presenting me with another situation, I see, in which the hard work we did on Saussurean theory is paying off. It's quite clear that four concepts we've mentioned relate to Snell's comparison: namely, paradigmatic/syntagmatic; and signification/value.

David Yes. Snell presents the following generalisation: 'Before he [Cicero] can attempt to phrase a philosophical concept without the article, he must borrow the content of the thought. His language, that is, becomes the receptacle of an element of meaning whose expression is more than its own unaided capacities will permit'. Snell, p. 228

This quotation involves one confusion, I feel. It arises precisely because Snell is not in command of the Saussurean concepts you've mentioned. While Snell **is** emphasising the different semantic consequences of different language systems, the wording of the quotation—with 'content' and 'element' of meaning—could be taken to imply that languages were just 'receptacles' for pre-existent meanings.

Paull   Maybe you're requiring too much of Snell's formulation in this case. It is obviously a difficult point to exemplify and explain. In fact, we have returned to a problem that concerned us earlier in this discussion—the difficulty of using a natural language to describe a natural language. Now, in the case of Malagasy and English, you emphasised how the interpretations changed depending on the point of view from which you begin, i.e., the English or the Malagasy. In the case of your quote from Snell, we have a three-way comparison: the words of English you offered to me described a difference between Greek and Latin.

David   Okay, and if I add that Snell's words were translated from German the situation is even more emphatic, isn't it?

Paull   Yes, of course. It is a case of relativity. No language offers the baseline for language or thought. I suppose one ought to be explicit then about the role of one's point of view.

David   I think you may have caught me out there, as regards to Snell, I mean. And your use of 'relativity' and point of view should become the theme of our next talk. With these concepts, I feel, one can summarise and integrate the diversity of sources in our present discussion. Furthermore, through point of view, one can see how directly all the issues of our discussions bear upon education.

So three matters need to be addressed in concluding this particular talk.
1   I should add one clarification to my comment on Snell's work. And by way of summary,
2   I would like to elaborate on your use of relativity. And by way of introducing our next talk,
3   I want to prefigure our arguments on point of view.

First of all, on Snell. To be fairer to his formulations, I should offer you a further brief quotation. In these words he not only throws light on the difficulties of talking about meaning, he elucidates the main problem of an evolutionary perspective on the intellect. And you'll recall that such a perspective is essential to Vygotsky's and Luria's description of Uzbekistan: the mind is not just 'affected' by socio-cultural conditions, it is 'effected' (made) by them.

Snell, p. viii

At this point we encounter two terminological difficulties. The first arises from a philosophical problem: in spite of our statement that the Greeks discovered the intellect we also assert that the discovery was necessary for the intellect to come into existence. Or, to put it grammatically: the intellect is not only an affective, but also an effective object. It must be obvious to anyone that we are here using a metaphor; but the metaphor is unavoidable, and is in fact the proper expression of what we have in mind. We cannot speak about the mind or the intellect at all without falling back on metaphor.

All other expressions, therefore, which we might employ to outline the situation, present the same difficulty. If we say that man understands himself or recognises himself, we do not mean the same thing as is meant by understanding an object, or recognising another man. For, in our use of the terms, the self does not come into being except through our comprehension of it.

Now the second point arises from your felicitous use of relativity.

All that we have encompassed in our two discussions so far can be justly regarded as preparation for your use of relativity—linguistic relativity. As you know, this last term is associated with the American linguist B.L. Whorf (1897–1941). It's my view that certain ideas need to be established before Whorf's theory can be appreciated. A list of these ideas can function as a review of our discussions.

Paull Again, it might be useful for me to try and list the topics we've discussed. What if I begin by simply calling our first talk the Saussurean legacy and then moving to this second discussion?

Overall, I would say our second talk has had two orientations. On the one hand, it has offered some illustrations of points implicit in the Saussurean theory of signs—in particular, it has brought out the problem of separating thought and language as if signs consisted only of *signifiants* (signifiers). Just as the relations between signs in a language are the basis of its phonological patterns, so too these relations are the basis for patterns of thought.

The other orientation mixes illustration and theory: the status of universals. This issue was provoked by comparisons of meaning systems, both across cultures and across groups within the one culture. Luria's sojourn in Uzbekistan was the main source of both forms of comparison. In considering universals we pursued matters like vision, the laws of logic, numerals, and the limits of empiricism in Heisenberg's physics. We also treated universals specifically related to language.

David Well, the claims here were of three kinds, I suppose. Those based on structure alone; those based on structure and mental organs; and those based on semantics. Of those based on semantics there are the 'atoms of meaning' theories, which are related to a *lingua mentalis*, and the functional theories, which are abstracted from forms of social activity.

Paull Now the last is in most ways antithetical to the other approaches: it is an inter-organism perspective, not an intra-organism one; and it emphasises contexts of situation and of culture—no particular meaning is a universal human endowment.

David Probably the only theme in our talk that needs to be further emphasised is the interdependence between the meaning potential of a culture and the possibilities of thought.

Paull I did refer to it; but it's certainly important enough to reiterate. The areas we discussed (through Luria's research) were perception, problem-solving, and the awareness of self. In each of these cases you suggested reasons to reject conventional assumptions, much in the same way as we rejected conventional assumptions about signs and correspondence. Vision is not a conduit but a form of thinking or making sense; the logic of a syllogism is not 'a priori' but depends on the status of report and hypothesis in the community; the individual 'self' is not given of consciousness but is an artefact of cultural evolution.

Also, a motif of our conversation has been the relativity involved in semantic description—the problems of operating without a legitimate meta-language.

The pluralism of reality

Richard Rorty, pp. 165–212

Nelson Goodman, *Ways of Worldmaking*, Harvester Press, Great Britain, 1978

David It would be more accurate to say that, actually, every language is **equally legitimate as a meta-language**. And this is the essence of linguistic relativity: when meanings can vary to the degree we have discussed, and when there is no 'privileged form of representation'—no repository of universally relevant meanings—then there is no **one** world and no **one** reality. Instead we are confronted with what Nelson Goodman calls different *Ways of Worldmaking*.

Different languages constitute different ways of making sense of experience. Goodman stresses that one cannot assume, even in principle, that different explanations of experience might be reduced to a single underlying reality (since the principles of reduction will also vary).

Paull I imagine that Whorf's theory is a precursor to Goodman's ideas . . .?

David Well, Goodman is not a linguist but a mathematician and logician. He discusses symbols from the perspective of the sciences and the 'languages of art'. On the other hand, Whorf's approach was to highlight the forms and consequences of different 'fashions of speaking'.

As with the study in Uzbekistan, Whorf's study of Hopi led him to connect ways of meaning with the habitual patterns of behaviour in a community; not with any species-specific, *lingua mentalis*. Whorf's own background in science—he was trained as a chemist before he worked as a linguist—prepared him for the metaphor of relativity. I think he took the metaphor very seriously and, as I suggested in our first talk, there is a direct analogy between certain problems of physics and certain problems in linguistics.

See pp. 8–9.

Whorf concentrated on what might be loosely called the metaphysical implications of linguistic differences. Hence, his discussions deal with different conceptions of time, the contrast between entity-ness and process-ness, and the place of *anima*, or thought if you like, in the scheme of phenomena. Whorf argues, that these were very significant differences between the Hopi cosmos and the cosmos of Europeans.

72

Paull Like many people with my interests, I have come across Whorf's theories but, I should add, they have been typically reported by psychologists or philosophers. In this form, they have been presented in terms of colour words, Eskimo words for snow, types of camels in desert communities, and so on.

David Yes, the Whorfian hypothesis is often discussed in terms of lexical items or words. This follows from the fact that words are the most obvious and/or manageable unit of a language. Also, those without the benefit of the Saussurean legacy tend to adopt a correspondence, referential view of language. This view, particularly when confined to 'words' and something vaguely called a 'sentence', provides no opportunity to comprehend the Whorfian concept 'fashions of speaking'. Whorf stresses in the following extract the concepts of 'time' and 'matter'.

> Concepts of 'time' and 'matter' are not given in substantially the same form by experience to all men but depend upon the nature of the language or languages through the use of which they have been developed. They do not depend so much upon ANY ONE SYSTEM (e.g. tense, or nouns) within the grammar as upon the ways of analysing and reporting experiences which have become fixed in the language as integrated 'fashions of speaking' and which cut across the typical grammatical classifications, so that such a 'fashion' may include lexical, morphological, syntactic, and otherwise systemically diverse means coordinated in a certain frame of consistency.
>
> Whorf, p. 158

Paull Well, I see that myself now; although I recall being vexed by Whorf's claims at different times in the past. It is plain that if one combines a referential theory of meaning with a 'mechanistic' theory of perception, there is absolutely no possibility of common ground with linguistic relativity. At most, I suppose, one would be confined to the weaker notion that different languages divide the 'same reality' in 'different' ways.

David And this certainly misses the point of Whorf, of Goodman, and anyone who holds that reality is constructed. There is no pantheon, no star chamber of the cosmos, to which we can appeal in order to legitimise one or other system of talking and thinking.

Accordingly, I think we must understand and utilise the pluralism of reality. This means, in the first instance, we must examine the intellectual structures—the referential theories of the sign or whatever—that obscure the pluralism or that make it invisible.

Paull Your idea of an obscured or invisible pluralism suddenly highlights a continuity in our talk, a thread that I only now see has run parallel to our concern with meaning systems. Whorf and Bernstein, for example, are proponents of the pluralism you've discussed. Both have tried to elucidate the diversity that goes unseen and unassessed. They have tried to bring out the consequences of different semantic systems. In Whorf's case the differences concern different background cultures. In the work of Bernstein the background of culture is constant, but different sub-groups make different sense of their experience.

Now it has emerged from our discourse that it is extremely difficult to 'see' differences of semantic orientation: as you noted earlier with respect to critics of Whorf, if one 'explains' a semantic difference it might then be dismissed on the very basis that it wasn't impossible to explain. Then again, if one can't explain a difference, authorities like Max Black claim that there is really nothing at issue.

David I agree. In fact Whorf's most important claims relate to what is called 'covert categories'. In our next talk I hope we can address the conundrum you have described, but in a way that shows how the pluralism of points of view, and of realities, bears on learning. I will argue that our own ideas of intellect relate to a covert phenomenon in the use of our language.

Discussion

A point of view

David At the beginning of our previous talk, Paull, you drew my attention to the role of 'object-ness' in analytical processes. You suggested that, in order to be objective, one really needed to be studying a 'thing'. You then went on to show how so many of the important objects of study were in fact not objects at all, but processes. In fact your examples of counselling and teaching might be called participatory processes—the analyst has to work both from within the phenomenon, while participating in it as an activity.

Paull Yes. I think our second talk could have made more of objectivity and education . . .

David It might help you to know that Whorf paid close attention to the way in which standard average European languages create 'things'. If we consider English, for example, there are considerable resources across the grammar for what is called nominalisation: operations whereby structures of various kinds can come to function like a nominal group within a single clause.

If I say, for example, 'The thing she really needs is some help around the house', then we have two clauses in the sentence: an outer clause and an inner or embedded clause. The whole sentence is the outer clause in this case. But the inner clause, *she really needs*, is not a subordinate clause in the traditional sense; rather it forms its primary relationship with a nominal group: *the thing*. In fact, the clause *she really needs* is part of that nominal group. We have a situation of rank-shift—a grammatical unit at one rank is made to function within a unit of a rank lower down, within a nominal group. Rank-shifted—or embedded—clauses can be indicated by brackets [ ].

Paull Now, what you called the 'rank-scale' was . . . sentence, clause, group, word, morpheme . . .?

David Yes. The significance of rank-shift becomes clearer when we think of the direct relationship between the nominal group and the concept of a thing or entity, a fact made explicit in our example. If a clause is (among other functions) the means of

Objectness and the nominal group

75

representing a process, it is clear that rank-shift is a resource for bringing processes into the encoding of 'thing-ness'.

Paull You are suggesting that 'process' can be in a way subsumed by the notion of an entity?

David At least in so far as certain kinds of linguistic configuration go with the idea of a 'thing'. For example, once you have encoded an event as a nominal group, it is then possible to attribute qualities to 'it'. And note, my use of 'it' indicates that a form of reification has taken place. Below is a sentence which illustrates this attribution:

> Dancing can be strenuous
> Folk dancing can be strenuous
> Scottish folk dancing can be strenuous

Paull This time you're not using rank-shift or embedding, are you? You have merely used the '-ing' form of the participle to make a nominal group; *dance* goes to *dancing* and then is given the modifying terms *folk* and *Scottish*. The item *strenuous* is the main attribute to which you were referring, I suppose. Now I can see a point to nominalising—once you have the nominal group you can bestow qualities on it. It gets back to my point about the relation between analysis and 'thing-hood'.

David Originally your point was, I feel, a negative one: in short, objective analysis seems to be more successful with things and isolated systems—these lend themselves to the measurements and predictions which legitimise the analysis in the judgment of the community at large. It's just that, as you emphasised, many of the most important phenomena of experience may not be tractable—they're not like things or isolated systems.

Paull Yes. A teacher lives all the time with relativity and indeterminacies. While a barrister might view his own achievements according to the success he brings to his clients, a teacher certainly can't judge his own performance by how many of his students pass the exam: many people pass their English exam despite being 'taught' to abhor poetry; many 'successful' mathematics students don't keep up their maths after their HSC exam.

David Okay. I don't doubt your point here. But I haven't any special insight I can offer you on these matters. What I do hope to clarify is an aspect of the intellect which is of fundamental importance to education at every level and age. My own judgment here depends on the clarifications we have worked out: from Saussure and the sign to the anti-Cartesian theories of Vygotsky and Luria.

Paull Could you perhaps outline the aspect of intellect which you are going to discuss? It would be helpful to have an idea of your destination, especially when I'm trying to see all our preceding discourse as one piece.

76

David   The destination is a theory about point of view and its role in the development of intellectual structures. One issue I want to argue is that our concept of intellect involves addressing point of view as an object.

Paull   I'm not sure this makes our goal all that much clearer. What do you mean by an object in this case? Obviously point of view cannot be an object of the same order as the objects which litter our lives. You are using object, then, in a special, maybe metaphoric, way . . .?

David   I'll explain what I mean by object. Let's begin though, by noting the degree to which the objects in our experience actually vary with respect to their order of abstraction. The general class of objects is not at all an unambiguous category—while trees, stones, horses, sun and moon appear to create no difficulties, many common objects of casual conversation are highly abstract. Think of 'the weather'; 'the government'; 'the education system'; 'the traffic'; 'business'; 'holidays'; 'public demand'; 'unemployment'; 'national defence'; 'the deficit'; 'inflation'; 'the news'; as well as more overt grammatical metaphors, e.g.,

'the likely outcome of the forthcoming elections'

Deictic Epithet Thing Qualifier [(prep.): Deictic Classifier Thing]

Figure 10

Now I know you will have a number of ways of explaining the special character of each of the above examples. But the point I am making is simply that all the nominal groups quoted here function as things or objects in the casual talk of our community. No speaker using them feels any need to apologise for being 'metaphoric'. And this is the case despite the generalisation in 'business' or the density of ideas in 'the likely outcome of . . . etc.

Paull   Yes. It's not just that *likely* and *forthcoming* complicate the things in the nominal group, the words *outcome* and *elections* are themselves problematic, aren't they?

David   Yes; in so far as they are forms of 'non-congruent' encoding. This is to say they are **not** the most direct way of encoding the processes they purport to represent: they are rather instances of 'happen' and 'elect'. But these two process items have taken on the structure typically associated with objects—both 'happen' and 'elect' have been encoded as nominal groups, as things rather than as processes.

M. A. K. Halliday, *An Introduction to Functional Grammar*, Edward Arnold, London, 1985.

Paull   The issue you are raising here reminds me of arguments which were presented by Quine. He stressed that the 'epistemological footing [of] physical objects and the gods [of Homer] differ only in degree and not in kind. Both sorts of entities enter our conception only as cultural posits'. I take Quine to be saying that the entities of our experience do not fall into simple sub-categories of physical and mental, concrete and abstract, certain and fictional, etc.

W. V. O. Quine, *From a Logical Point of View*, Harper Torchbooks, New York, 1963, p. 44

David   Yes; and this brings our talk back to objects and how one might speak of point of view as an object. You see, I want to argue that we ought to interpret the orientation of our language system as a positive resource, not just as the origin of possible limitations in our potential to mean. Note here, I used two concepts central to the work of the systemic linguists who have contributed to this course: the idea of language as a positive 'resource'; and the term 'meaning potential'.

Paull   What, though, **is** the orientation of our language system? The nominalising and objectifying operations which we have just discussed—are they the orientation?

David   They certainly reflect the orientation. The considerable powers of nominalisation in English are very important for speakers and writers. Yet there has been a tendency amongst some advanced thinkers to highlight consequences of nominalisation which could be regarded as negative.

Paull   Maybe you could review these 'negative' consequences. I see how my comments about studying processes (and **not** things) might be seen as negative. But I am not clear how nominalisation tells me anything about my own intellectual predicament.

Philosophers and 'misplaced concreteness'

David   We can begin by reviewing the kinds of observations which have been made with respect to objectification in English (and other European languages). Specialists in many fields, not just in linguistics, have commented on the constraints experienced trying to express the concepts of their disciplines through the grammatical structures of English.

The grammatical structure most often cited as a source of difficulty is the relationship between 'subject and predicate'. What is at issue, essentially, is the notion that our language represents experience according to a two-part division—as if there were, on the one hand: **things**, and on the other: **events**, **actions**, or **properties** in which the things are involved. Whorf actually referred to this two-part division of reality as an 'ideology'.

Whorf, p. 241

Paull   I imagine that the crucial factor in the ideology is that things must always precede events, or attributes, or relations.

David   Yes. This is one aspect of the ideology which Whorf singled out for criticism. And if you think back to the way the sign was discussed by Saussure—totally in terms of relations—you can see how a two-part division between things and events/relations/ properties can be misleading. We can see that in language the entities **do not** precede relations; just as we found that thoughts as signifieds, cannot be regarded as prior to their signifiers.

Paull   In what other fields has research been limited by the subject-predicate form of encoding?

David   In order to fill out what I am calling the negative case, I'll offer one instance from each of philosophy, physics, and the life

78

sciences. Note, I am recounting to you particular claims that have been made. I am not implying that these views amount to the most widely accepted interpretations in each particular subject—far from it. But these comments on the subject-predicate structure in English (and that structure's association with 'thing-hood') do come from thinkers who have long worked at the very limits of their discipline. I am referring to A.N. Whitehead in philosophy, D. Bohm in physics, and the biologist C.H. Waddington.

Whitehead's philosophy is often referred to as a process philosophy. It involves, therefore, an inversion of our tendency to emphasise the fixity of things. In his most important philosophical tract, *Process and Reality*, Whitehead both repudiates the 'subject-predicate form of expression' and criticises other philosophers for slipping into 'subject-predicate habits of thought'. His approach reinterprets entities as 'occasions of experience'.

A. N. Whitehead, *Process and Reality*, Cambridge University Press, London, 1929, p. viii

Whitehead, p. 70. See also pp. 103, 192, 201, 221, 313.

Like Whitehead, Bohm emphasises the interconnectedness of all aspects of the cosmos. In fact, both men share a relational view of reality. Bohm explores how one can come to see the order which may be implicit in 'apparent' disorder. And, specifically with regard to language, Bohm makes some attempt at devising a linguistic mechanism—the RHEOMODE—by which processness can be genuinely expressed.

In Waddington's *Tools for Thought*, the biologist discussed ways of representing information which emphasise 'the process character of things'. Citing Whitehead, Waddington goes on to mention the way all observations are kinds of experiments; and how these experiments can lead to the 'fallacy of misplaced concreteness'—when abstract notions are derived from actual occasions of experience and then treated as if they could 'be picked up and placed somewhere else'.

C. H. Waddington, *Tools for Thought*, Paladin, Herts, 1977, p. 22

Waddington, p. 24

Paull Well, I would just like to clarify where we are in our discussion. You are giving me support, aren't you, in my view of education? You are showing that objectivity is really only compatible with objects, and this fact can be discerned in a number of disciplines. Human or social sciences are like the process philosophies you've mentioned in that they lack a method or a meta-language for extracting the salient aspects of interactive processes.

Education and social sciences

David That's not quite right, is it? In general a science like psychology has a considerable tradition of methods and conventions, but . . .

Paull But they reflect what I mentioned earlier (when we first began to discuss perception); namely, the tendency of researchers to mimic the approaches of the physical sciences—in part, perhaps, to guarantee rigour; but also to establish their place according to the canonical view of objectivity in science.

David   Yes. We touched on this in the first talk in conjunction with atomism and reductionism.

Paull   Now that you have drawn my attention to problems and methods in the study of language, I am even more deeply struck by the uneasy place of education. It appears that, as a subject studied at tertiary level, education adopts many of its issues and methods from psychology; and of course from sociology. The things studied in education are essentially the things that already concern psychologists, for example, cognition.

I wonder whether educationists shouldn't have given more attention to phenomena and methods which are peculiar to education. I am suggesting this in the same way that one might wonder whether psychology should have been less concerned with emulating the methods of the physical sciences.

David   I can't resist expressing a view here, although I note that our main topic is the objectification of point of view.

The relation between education and linguistics might be helpful in clarifying your suggestions concerning education and psychology. I can't see anything to be gained by educationists turning their backs on linguistics—quite the opposite. Similarly, it stands to reason that educationists will share many research interests with psychologists. But, returning to linguistics, it is important that educationists demand a model, a description of language, which meets their own problems and experience squarely. The difficulties in the study of language indicate that one cannot underrate the specialists. Nevertheless, one must be sure that the specialists encompass the educationists' experience of language, and not some attenuated, shadowy substitute.

Bringing my own statements down to earth somewhat: it seems clear that to be relevant to educational contexts, a theory of language would need to—
1   address texts and not merely sentences;
2   differentiate between text forms or generic structures;
3   be explicit about the role of contexts in controlling the appropriateness of meanings;
4   clarify the factors involved in switching mode from spoken to written; . . . and so on . . .

Paull   In bringing the linguist to confront the educationist's experience of language, the educationist has as much to offer the specialist as the specialist has to offer the educationist.

David   I don't doubt that for one minute. One has only to reflect on the narrow views on child language development prevalent just a few years ago. It was not uncommon to read work which assumed that all children do their language learning between the years of two and four (as if they go from virtually nothing to 'mastery' in that period). Teaching is, as you say, a participatory process. Certainly, no aspect of it is going to be better understood without the participation of its participants.

But let's return to the question of point of view and nominalisation. At this stage, we have looked at some negative interpretations of nominalisation and of the 'thingness' implicit in subject-predicate structures. Whorf, Whitehead, Bohm and Waddington—they all state that, in some respects, our world would be more coherent if we could move beyond the 'subject-predicate habits of thought'.

Whitehead, p. 70

If we think about Halliday's concept of language as a 'resource', it might lead us to ask about the positive aspects to the 'habits' criticised by Whitehead. Are there, for example, interpersonal or textual functions that should be considered?

Paull   I shouldn't discount the chance that an orientation to thingness has consequences that I am unable to see; I mean benefits even with respect to Halliday's experiential function.

David   From your last comment I want to proceed with my argument concerning point of view and objectification. Given that point of view is an interpersonal phenomenon, my observations will ultimately include that meta-function in the grammar. The important textual consequences of nominalisations, I won't be treating specifically. These relate, in particular, to the organisation of the message into theme and rheme; and they can be found in Halliday's *Introduction to Functional Grammar*.

Halliday, *An Introduction to Functional Grammar*

Paull   How would you argue, then, for positive consequences to our tendency to reify, to turn our experience into 'things'?

David   It may surprise you when I say that the philosopher Nietzsche had a most accurate and balanced view of the way humans create 'fictions'. Of course, by fiction here, Nietzsche meant something like a construct of the intellect—something hypothetical or heuristic. In fact Nietzsche occasionally uses the word in a way similar to Richard Gregory's use of hypothesis and fiction.

The philosophy of 'as if'

See previous discussion, pp. 43–4.

Paull   Was Nietzsche the originator of this use of fiction?

David   No. He, too, was part of a tradition. This tradition was described, in 1924, in a study by Hans Vaihinger: *The Philosophy of 'As If'*.

Paull   I take it that 'as if' is an indication that the philosophy concerned makes use of hypothetical models?

Hans Vaihinger, *The Philosophy of 'As If'*, (tr.) C. K. Ogden, Harcourt, Brace & Company, New York, 1925, p. 352

David   For Nietzsche truth was a special use of metaphors. He emphasised—like Goodman more recently—that all experience involves perspective forms: the perspective is 'the basic condition of all life'.

Furthermore, Nietzsche stressed what could be called a semiotic view of reality: humans read their 'sign-world into things as something really existing' and when we do this 'we are merely doing what we have always done, namely mythologising'.

Vaihinger, p. 354

Paull   So the terms fiction and myth overlap here?

David   Yes, they do. But the crucial point Nietzsche develops concerns the importance of fictions and myths. They are 'necessary' to life.

Paull   What range of concepts does he classify as fictions?

David   Well oppositions like cause-effect, subject-object, means-end; concepts like compulsion, number, law, logical thinking, freedom; also points, lines . . . and so on. Virtually all that is generally regarded as abstract as well as the ideas which are often considered to be a priori.

Nietzsche's method is exemplified by his observations on logic. He describes it as 'a consistent sign-language worked out on the assumption of the existence of identical cases . . . that identical things and identical cases exist is the basic fiction, first in judgment and then in inference'.

Paull   So logic develops only because one has already accepted the fiction of identical things?

David   Yes. But accepting such fictions, making use of the hypothetical, even introducing illusion, are part of bringing order into the world: 'the fictional world of subject, substance, reason, etc., is necessary'.

Nevertheless, on the issue we've discussed with respect to Whorf, Whitehead, et al, Nietzsche is also quite explicit: 'there is no substratum, there is no 'being' behind the action, behind the 'action on', behind the becoming; the 'agent' has been merely read into the action—the action is all there is . . .'

Paull   I gather, from Nietzsche's idea of fictions, that our sign systems create entities; and that these entities are important because they bring order and form to human experience. In his usual way, Nietzsche dramatises the situation by suggesting they are kinds of necessary falsehood.

David   That's true. But I believe the situation does merit the dramatisation. There are two components to Nietzsche's argument. In the first place he is stressing the fact of perspective—that experience is always **from a particular point of view.** Secondly, he is arguing that our 'sign-world' supplies the essential order of experience, albeit a fictional order.

Paull   I concede that these two issues have dramatic implications for thinking. But I still need to be clearer on their significance for education.

David   The reifications in our talk, the 'things' constructed, become the subject-matter of educational discourse. This can be seen by reflecting on Nietzsche's inventory of fictions: from cause and effect (which he associated with an erroneous conception of subject and predicate) to the 'objects of mathematics'. But seeing our curricula as interlocking fictions is not my central concern.

In talking out these issues with you, Paull, over our three discussions, a number of seemingly disparate elements have become for me a single line of consistency.

Paull   Well, what were the disparate elements? Or is it best for me to arrive at the consistency by working my own way to them?

Vaihinger, p. 356

Vaihinger, p. 359

Vaihinger, p. 354

Vaihinger, p. 352

David All right. Yes. That might be the best approach.

Now the ideas that stand out for me represent a kind of global summary of our talks:

1 Relations.
2 Reality as construct.
3 Reality as artefact.

Paull Point (1) looks back to our discussion of Saussure. Point (2) refers to the issues surrounding Luria's visit to Uzbekistan. And (3) is . . . well (3) is not so straightforward.

David Point (3) covers our discussion of 'heuristic fictions'—the ideas which are important cultural tools but which, at bottom, have an 'as if' character.

Paull But why call them 'artefacts'? They are constructs just like any other idea we've discussed.

David Yes. But what I'm trying to bring out is the added feature of deliberation or self-consciousness concerning these constructs. This seems to be the particular force of Nietzsche's observations —one is asked to live with a sense of the fabrication of reality, of reality as a fabric of signs.

The 'single line of consistency' to which I referred, however, involves two further concepts: text and point of view. Text has been treated in depth by the Halliday and Hasan book *Language, Context and Text*. For my purposes I need only draw your attention to the ensemble of relations in a text and the fact that texts ultimately derive their meanings from the social processes in which they are involved—their 'contexts of situation'.

David The meaning of point of view, for me, subsumes all of the following: 'observer' in physics, 'perspective form' in Nietzsche's philosophy; 'frame of reference' as discussed in Goodman's *Ways of Worldmaking*, as well as the conventional notion in literary studies, e.g., the point of view of a particular narrative.

Point of view: its meaning and grammar
Goodman, pp. 3-4

Related to the uses listed here, there are also systems of lexico-grammatical choice which are directly or indirectly relevant to the expression of one's specific angle on experience.

The foremost of these is the system of modality. Through modality one can encode all the range of meanings between a positive *yes* and an unequivocal *no*, as well as the frequency or unusualness of an event. This range of meanings is realised through the verbal group—may, might, could, would, etc., or in various other ways:

1 by modal adjuncts: possibly, probably, often . . .
2 by clause-like structures: I think, it's possible that . . .

There are other lexico-grammatical forms related to point of view, but which are not quite so obvious in their semantic relevance:

The system is extensive, and for a full review refer to Halliday, *An Introduction to Functional Grammar*.

1 the expression of conditions—'if' clauses . . .;
2 the various means by which one reports on the sayings and meanings of **other people**; and,

3   the ways by which one expresses the reactions and
perceptions of different individuals, including oneself.

Paull   So you've outlined three main areas. In fact, according to
your account, there are three general types of meaning involved
in point of view. There's the speaker's angle on 'yes/no' and
'how often'. That seems also to include conditions (. . .'if',
etc.). Secondly, there is the report of what others have said or
thought. And third, there is the report of reactions and
perceptions—though, from what we said about perception in our
second discussion, it may be difficult to support a notional
difference between what is thought and the process of
perceiving.

David   Well, I'd agree with that. But your summary is very useful
because it brings out an issue that can go unnoticed: namely, that
part of the job of expressing one's own point of view is being
clear on the views of others.

Paull   Okay. And there is an interesting irony in this—individuality
implies membership of a group. It is an issue emphasised by
Gregory Bateson: for example, 'aggression' is not an individual
characteristic; it is rather the characteristic of a person's
interaction with others. Many terms make no sense at all when
used as if they were attributes of isolated individuals.

David   I think you're right. Our individual thoughts and points of
view are ultimately derived from our participation in the system.

This brings us, however, to the major issue I wanted to put
before you. Perhaps I should express it in summary as briefly as
I can; and then we can reconsider it in a more detailed way.

Paull   Well, I might have come to it already: being clear about
one's own angle on things (in relation to the views of others) is
a broad statement of what goes on in learning. It is, of course,
too broad to explain much. What I have noted, however, right
throughout my experience of the education system, is that the
most successful students—the ones who are typically associated
with great intellectual promise are the ones who appear to have a
natural facility for turning back and examining their own point of
view as if it were itself the object of study. In a sense, they are
always working on the role of the self in relation to certain types
of goings on . . . goings on with narrative, with numbers, with
objective experiments and so forth, depending on what one calls
the activity (i.e., English, maths, science).

David   Yes, you've certainly beaten me to my destination. The
most general character of intellectual endeavour, at least as we
were brought up to identify it, appears to be a turning back and
making one's own perspective the very subject matter of
enquiry. Such a strategy to learning is something like observing
yourself as observer.

This may sound a sterile, narcissistic approach when expressed
in such simple terms. But I will try to elaborate on the strategy
in three contexts. First, I'll exemplify it in what I believe is its
quintessential form in our culture. Second, I will draw on our

discussion of the lexico-grammar of point of view in order to relate the strategy to the development of language in the young child. Third, I'll offer some more general observations on how point of view becomes a crucial aspect of high school and tertiary education.

Just two aspects of your account, in my view, need reconsideration. Your use of '**natural** facility' is unjustified. I hope to show that the orientation to meaning which you've described can be followed back to the patterns of meaning in the family.

The second comment is not a criticism; merely a reminder that you spoke of point of view as an object of study. In other words, we have returned to our discussion of 'thing-ness', albeit through a more positive example.

Paull Well, I agree with these observations. So what **are** the quintessential forms in our culture?

David I suppose I could reach in a number of directions for illustrations. But the domain which I personally have been able to penetrate to greatest depth is the grammatical structure of poetry. Two short examples from the poetry of Wallace Stevens will be sufficient. They will indicate how subtle the examination of point of view has become. Both the short texts were written around 1920. The poet himself, who died in 1955, is often regarded as the mysterious, 'difficult' giant of modern poetry.

Let's take the first of the poems, 'Tattoo', and discuss it briefly before moving on to 'The Load of Sugar-cane'.

Point of view: its textual construction

Tattoo

Sc.1	I	The light is like a spider.		1α
Sc.2	II	It crawls over the water.		1α
Sc.3	III	It crawls over the edges of the snow.		1α
Sc.4	IV	It crawls under your eyelids	$1\alpha\ ^+ 2\alpha\ ^+ 3\alpha$	
	V	And spreads its web there—		
	VI	Its two webs.		
Sc.5	VII	The webs of your eyes		α
	VIII	Are fastened		$\varkappa$
	IX	To the flesh and bones of you		β
	X	As to rafters or grass.		
Sc.6	XI	There are filaments of your eyes		1α
	XII	On the surface of the water		
	XIII	And in the edges of the snow.		

Wallace Stevens, 'Tattoo' and 'The Load of Sugar-Cane', in *The Collected Poems of Wallace Stevens*, Faber and Faber, London, 1955

The wording of the poem is framed by (a) the number of each sentence (e.g., Sc.1); (b) the line number (I, II, III . . .); and (c) the clause complex description (e.g., 1α). From the page then, one can read off information like the following: Sentence 4 includes lines IV, V, and VI and consists of a clause complex of three paratactic clauses (related to one another as forms of extension $(+)$).

Now if we reflect on the function of a clause, an interesting aspect of this poem begins to emerge. A clause is the unit which models processes—at least, this is one of its functions.

Paull   I had thought that verbs were the means of expressing processes.

David   Actually 'verb' is a class term, not a genuine description of a function. Nevertheless, you can see that processes in English are represented by a configuration (not merely a single term). So, with respect to material processes, one might have a configuration of actor-process-goal-recipient, etc.

Paull   An interesting point about the poem is that its subject matter concerns perception—a mental process. It appears to track the passage of light into the eyes and the neurones of the brain. My interest is aroused here because I'm used to thinking of vision as a unitary, almost instantaneous event. In this poem, vision is slow and incremental.

David   I agree. What's more, the increment appears to have two directions. Up to line X the light is an actor, crawling into the eye and spreading; while in lines XI—XIII, egressive light—the *filaments of your eyes*—extends to the water and snow.

Halliday, *An Introduction to Functional Grammar*

But your point about increment is the more important. Seeing is presented as a series of discrete stages. The textual mechanism for achieving this is simple: since a clause models a process, if one presents an event as a number of clauses, then it follows that **the event is being seen as a number of processes**. The significance of this explanation becomes clearer as we contrast 'Tattoo' with the second poem.

Wallace Stevens, 'The Load of Sugar-Cane'

The Load of Sugar-Cane

I   The going of the glade-boat
II   Is like water flowing;

III   Like water flowing
IV   Through the green saw-grass;
V   Under the rainbows;

VI   Under the rainbows
VII   That are like birds,
VIII   Turning, bedizened,
IX   While the wind still whistles
X   As kildeer do,

XI   When they rise
XII   At the red turban
XIII   Of the boatman.

Paull   A brief overview suggests to me that there is a similar structure in this poem, although its effect on me as a reader is curious. This is to say the poem looks like five simple chunks of information, each one merely adding to the aggregate. I used the word 'curious', however, because at the end of the poem, the reader discovers that he is back where he started—back with the *boat*. You think the subject-matter has changed or moved along; then you glean that all the similes of the text are presenting *the glade-boat* of line 1.

David   Yes. This poem also deals with seeing or, more accurately, with points of view. There are the observations of lines 1—X; and then the perspective of the small birds (the *kildeer*) amidst the marsh grass (lines XI—XIII).

Paull   But the 'seeing' in 'The Load of Sugar-Cane' is not an incremental process, is it?

David   Well, it begins with a series of additions; but then there is a sea change precisely at the poem's mid-point—at line VII *That are like birds*.

What the reader encounters at line VII is embedding. But it extends from that point right to the end of the poem. So the material in lines VII—XIII actually all functions within the nominal group *the rainbows* . . .

This is set out in figure 11.

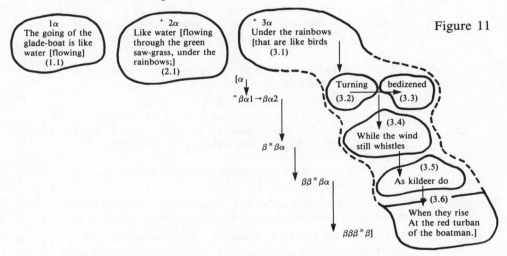

Figure 11

Paull   What does the arrangement signify here? What are the three encircled bits: $1\alpha + 2\alpha + 3\alpha$ . . .?

David   They are the three additive clauses. Note, of course, that 2α and 3α involve ellipsis.

Paull   Why then is 3α dotted and curving down? I remember that the [ ] brackets indicate an embedded clause. But what's happened in 3α?

David   After *the rainbows* the clauses are embedded. That is, they constitute an embedded clause complex. Now with the clause complex, hypotactic relationships are displayed by 'β' symbols and the downwardness or depth of the clause with respect to its main clause (i.e. the 'α' clause). Paratactic relationships are rendered by numbering the clauses at the same level on the

Halliday & Hasan,
Language, Context and Text

87

diagram. So clauses 3.2 and 3.3 correspond to the descriptions $\beta\alpha1 \rightarrow \beta\alpha2$: they are the 1st and 2nd clauses at the single 'β' depth, within the embedding.

Paull   I see—you are describing *Turning, bedizened* as two clauses at the same depth within the extended embedding of 3α . . .

David   Yes.

Paull   The structure of this poem turns out to be very different then from the organisation of 'Tattoo'. But what does the difference mean?

David   Well, such structural differences in a text always have semantic consequences. In this case the difference of meaning relates to our discussions of 'thing-ness' and of point of view.

I suggested that these poems are powerful illustrations of how point of view can become the subject matter, even the object, of enquiry. In 'Tattoo', vision is constructed as a sum of discrete events. On the other hand, experience in 'The Load of Sugar-Cane' is organised around attribution (*is like*) and around a nominal expression that subsumes a number of processes. The *rainbows* . . . becomes a complex thing, with the events (*Turning, whistles, rise* . . .) as part of the specification of that thing.

Paull   So the two poems taken together amount to different ways of modelling point of view?

David   Yes. I think that's right: different perspectives have been constructed. What I have brought to your attention concerning the clauses in each poem ought to be developed to show how the poet organises many different kinds of relationships into an ensemble.

But we have taken the poems as far as is needed in the present discussion.

Paull   They were instances, you claimed, of a turning-back to make one's own perspective the very subject matter of enquiry.

David   Yes, and I have emphasised this turning-back—this reflexive enquiry— because it seems to me the source of so much that we value as 'thinking'. For example, I become conscious of my 'self' by constructing my own angle on the world—my point of view as distinct from the experience of others.

Paull   This would bring you to your second point, I imagine. You were going to relate point of view to child language development —how this reflexive enquiry arises for an individual.

A child's view: from dialogue to hypothesis

David   Yes. Let me offer you an extract from a dialogue, a dialogue between myself and a child aged four years and ten months (4.10). These exchanges are part of a wider, two-phase project undertaken by Ruqaiya Hasan, with the aid of Carmel Cloran at Macquarie University. The project is relevant to our discussions of 'talking and thinking' since it is investigating 'the role of talk in establishing ways of learning'. The research is

88

centred on natural recordings of mother-child talk (around the homes when the children were about 3.10) and of talk at school during kindergarten (4.9—5.10). The samples below, however, come from a talk with one of the children just as that child had begun attending school.

In the backyard

(Child = Ch.; David = D)

Ch   Oh well, I only very [1] occasionally water this and it's growing very well.

D   Yes . . . it's got beautiful gum showing from it, hasn't it?

Ch   Mm. . . [2] Sometimes I climb it because it's alright; but not in a special dress or in my uniform—no. . . because [3] Mummy would smack me [4] if I went in my uniform.

D   I guess she would.

Ch   Mm.

D   Would she be upset if she had to do all the washing when you just climbed a tree?

Ch   Yeah . . . [5] might get a few threads out.

D   Oh well, that can happen, can't it: you can rip your uniform?

Ch   Mummy sticks [6] my hankie in here, and when I'm older and maybe [7] if we're still here she'll stick my bus money in it, when I'm older.

D   Yes. Is it a long way to school?

Ch   Oh no, it's not too . . . We had a choice of up, up the . . . where you cross a busy road or, no, [8] Mum wouldn't want that; or um, the one there that I go to. And we chose that one because that didn't have a busy road.

D   Right next to it. . . .?

Ch   Yes . . . No, it wasn't right next to it. The [9] one that has a busy road was next to the kinder that I went to that Elsie's gonna go to.

Paull   What are the numbers? Single features that relate to point of view?

David   Well, let me be precise about your use of 'features'. I am not going to argue that the presence or absence of a particular lexico-grammatical form has one and only one semantic consequence. What I want to bring out is the pattern of consistency across this child's talk—the semantic pattern. Hasan emphasises in her own work that it is orientation to meaning that needs to be clarified. The significance of a lexico-grammatical choice is derived from the place of the choice amidst the ensemble of choices in the text. So, for example, consider the last sentence of the dialogue (see 9). It has an embedded clause and an embedded clause complex: *The one* [that. . .] *was next to the kinder* [that . . . that . . .].

Paull   I think I can see the explanation for this structure—the embedding enables the child to arrange the message in accordance with her main concerns: *The one that has a busy road* becomes the theme.

David And the message becomes a single relational clause of circumstance (since the embedded clauses are part of their respective nominal groups *the one* . . . and *the kinder* . . .). So, while I have previously stressed the experiential consequences of nominalisation, there are many reasons why a speaker might embed a process in a nominal group. And these reasons are not peculiar to one kind of subject matter or one kind of language user.

Paull But you were saying that a number of choices could be seen as constituting a pattern. As I understood you, the semantic pattern is a consistency of choice—a tendency.

David Yes, and this is where the numbers 1—8 are relevant. Already in this child's discourse considerable attention is given to specifying point of view: what is her judgment, her reaction, and her habit of behaviour (see 1, 2, 5, 6). Furthermore, the point of view of others is reported—in 8 we find a report of an opinion actually expressed by the mum; while in 3 to 4 and 7 the child presents hypothetical cases, happenings dependent on conditions (*if I* . . . ; . . . *maybe if* . . .).

Paull The numbers 1 to 8 then, indicate the lexico-grammatical forms which you see as a pattern in this child's meanings.

David The consistency reveals an orientation to meaning. This exchange is representative of this child's approach to topics as diverse as lizards, shopping, and school.

Paull Wouldn't all these forms be present in the talk of most, if not all, normal children; though to a lesser degree. . .?

David I would think so, but that is one of the issues we've discussed in these sessions. One cannot judge different orientations to meaning on the basis of the presence or absence of a particular form: e.g. + modality. It is the quest for peculiar, definitive forms that has led to so many misunderstandings: for instance, researchers have typically discussed the work of both Whorf and Bernstein in terms of some kind of concrete marker at the level of lexico-grammar. The theories of these men, however, are concerned with far more subtle phenomena—a principle of organisation at the level of semantics.

Now I have suggested that a certain orientation to meaning is a central strategy for developing the patterns of thinking in our culture.

Paull Okay, the turning-back on point of view—treating point of view as the object of enquiry.

David In the case of the child discussed above, the lexico-grammatical resources related to point of view are clearly established. But, what's more, a certain consistency of meaning is also established. This pattern has a number of strands:

1 my views and feelings;
2 Mum's views and feelings;

3 other views and feelings (little sister, Dad. . .);

4 other sayings, thoughts, and facts;

5 hypothetical states of affairs (the 'as if'. . .).

Paull You are implying that this child is already well oriented for the kinds of demands that the educational system will make upon her. She is already demarcating points of view and different objects of thought.

David First of all, she is very much concerned with objects of thought: in particular, with verbal and mental projections. It is as if there is incipient in her talk, a level which is typically associated with higher education: namely, a level from which the entities created by talking and thinking are accorded a status difficult to distinguish from the 'objectivity' of water, earth, fire, and air.

This child is, I feel, well oriented for the demands that the educational system will make upon her; at least in so far as we are discussing curricula or subject areas. This little girl is well on her way to making sense of demands like 'Explain the role of the narrator in the novel _____', or 'Explain the differences between China and Britain which brought about the Opium wars'. Similarly, she is preparing herself to operate with meta-phenomena like π, $\sqrt{2}$, 'molecular structure', 'light years', and so on . . . In fact, it won't surprise you to learn that the child's mother is herself a teacher, and that the pattern of talk in the extract reflects a pattern of elaboration habitual to the home.

Paull Well, what kind of abstractions might the child be managing herself at this stage, that is, at the stage of just beginning school?

David In general, I would say the abstractions that have been functional in the discourse of the home . . . Clearly, I am trying to dodge any suggestion that a five-year-old should talk according to 'this' pattern or 'that'. But, here is an example from another girl who has just entered school. It shows the degree to which a small child may have talked her way into an abstract, syllogistic mode—the mode that was so alien to the talk of many Uzbeks.

The mother and child are sitting together in this exchange. The daughter makes the comment that she hates school, a comment which contradicts her usual statements about school. The mother then decides to ask the child about her teacher, knowing that this is likely to bring out her general enjoyment of school:

Mum: Do you hate Mrs McDonald?
Child: Do I hate my family?!!
I'd hate you if I hated her.
Do you hear that?
Cause I love her.
Do you hear that?
I'd have to hate you!

Paull Yes, I can see that there is a great deal compressed into this outburst: in so much as the girl's reaction to her teacher is of the same category as her feelings towards her mother, if her feelings to her teacher were in fact hate (which they are not), then it would follow that the feelings towards the mother would be hate. This is to say A and B are the same with respect to factor C; if the reaction A/C is changed then the relationship B/C is changed in the same way.

David Yes. Note that the whole issue is hypothetical or heuristic. So too, it rests on a principle we discussed with respect to Nietzsche—the fiction of equivalent cases. And thirdly, the *I'd have to hate you* in the final clause indicates that the child is drawing attention to a form of logical imperative in the whole fabrication: as if the consequence, hating mum, would be a logical necessity (almost something beyond the influence of the child's own feelings or volition).

I think this example reveals the child in the process of constructing 'reason'. Her argument is already an appeal to an impersonal structure that exists outside her: she has become an agent forced into hating because of the objective nature of the connections between facts.

Paull Yes. She is claiming that all this follows from the nature of things, or rather 'facts' (as you said). Expressing this in Popperian terms, it would be that the world 2 (her thoughts and feelings) were under the constraint of world 3 (the construct of the mind). Of course, she is overstating the situation for rhetorical effect.

David Well, I think you have uncovered a very important dimension of the exchange. The argument or reasoning is unacceptable. Yet it has considerable interpersonal force. I would suggest, then, that the motivation behind the child's fabrication is interpersonal (at least in the first place). Naturally, the uses of hypothesis and reasoning can take on a life of their own. And, while I certainly don't want to imply that they have no genuine ideational function in the child's argument, one ought to give appropriate emphasis to the likelihood that our logical constructs are interpersonal in origin.

This is tantamount to saying that the language we use for reflecting on the world is taken over from our resources for managing interaction.

Paull This is merely conjectural, isn't it? One doesn't have access to how these processes arise in a culture.

David It would seem that you're right. But this kind of issue can be studied in the discourse of children, as in the present case.

Paull There is one point I would like to make concerning point of view and children. You emphasised the role of point of view as both theme and subject-matter in the poetry of Wallace Stevens. I feel that a related phenomenon occurs in children's books.

One example immediately comes to mind—it's an illustration. In *Turramulli the Giant Quinkin*, Percy Trezise and Dick Roughsey present an Aboriginal narrative about two children escaping a dangerous giant. Now the most effective illustration is a picture of Turramulli's feet passing a hollow log—that is, we are sharing the point of view of the two children who are hidden in the hollow log.

Percy Trezise and Dick Roughsey, *Turramulli the Giant Quinkin*, Collins, Sydney, 1982

David   Yes. I can think of many similar dramatisations of point of view—we are not looking at the happening; rather we come to share the perspective of a participant. *Aktil's Big Swim* is about a mouse who swims the English channel. Similarly in that book, the illustrations make dramatic use of the point of view of the fish, and also the perspective of the sea-gulls. I suppose this is related to what we discussed in the textual strategy of 'The Load of Sugar-Cane' (with the perspective of the kildeer).

Inga Moore, *Aktils Big Swim*, Oxford University Press, Melbourne, 1980

Now we've mentioned very young children, and also we've touched on the subjects of secondary education. What about tertiary education? The role of point of view seems even more overt at the tertiary level. My impressions are a result of teaching subjects as diverse as semantics, poetry, and Middle English. There is one student reaction which I feel is common across these discipline boundaries. A great many of the students who discussed their work with me were having difficulty locating their own view on an academic issue. Typically they did have a definite view. Only it was latent, or implicit. And they had to learn to ask questions **of themselves** in conjunction with texts from the discipline.

Paull   Yes. I've experienced that, and heard that, myself: it's quite common to hear a student say 'Oh yes. I can see what's required now—it's just that it didn't strike me while I was doing the assignment!' This is to say, the student is disappointed at not seeing what was accessible to him all along: his own role as interpreter of the subject.

David   There is one further thing I feel needs stressing. The experience of Luria in Uzbekistan suggests to me that 'talking and thinking' can take many forms. There is no reason to assume that one pattern or orientation is more legitimate than any other. Nevertheless with respect to a given purpose, we might agree on criteria by which these patterns of behaviour can be judged. It is in the context of particular purposes that we can interpret Luria's view of graphic-functional thinking. He seems to have regarded it as a socio-historical stage beyond which a culture must develop. At least, he stressed the positive, revolutionary consequences of creating 'objects of thought'.

Paull   Yes. I found the following comment on language in Luria's *Cognitive Development*:

Luria, *Cognitive Development*, p. 10

> . . . humans have at their disposal a powerful objective tool that permits them not only to reflect individual objects or situations but to create objective logical codes. Such codes enable a person to go beyond direct experience and to draw conclusions that have the

same objectivity as the data of direct sensory experience. In other words, social history has established the system of language and logical codes that permit men to make the leap from the sensory to the rational; for the founders of materialistic philosophy, this transition was as important as that from non-living to living matter.

One aspect of rationalism

David In my interpretation, these rational objects have their origin in a meta-level of talk. The meta-level may have arisen in our culture when the meaning potential of a particular community facilitated the kind of reflexive enquiry which we associate with Greek philosophy and the maxim 'know thyself'. Our discussion of Snell's work ought to be reconsidered here. But for me, not having Snell's access to Ancient Greek, the cultural origins of Western 'rationalism' will always be an obscure, though absorbing, issue.

On the other hand, this 'meta-level of talk' develops anew with each child. And here I do have direct access, just like any parent or teacher. As long as one is trained to discern the structure of the goings on—the patterns in the linguistic behaviour—the child can be observed in the process of constructing a world of opinions, facts, reports, reactions, perceptions, thoughts, hypotheses, and practical fictions.

This 'world' is **not** added to a primary world of trees, stones, and people. Rather the rational objects provide the principles by which the child extends and renovates his experience of phenomena. This is why the distinction between mental and phenomenal is so difficult to establish in any given instance— what we have learnt to call phenomena is worked out in conjunction with our resources for talking and thinking.

This world of projections: reports, opinion, hypotheses, and fictions, emerges when the child begins to distinguish points of view. A crucial aspect of education begins when point of view takes on an ideational significance as well as its interpersonal function—when the child begins to treat her or his own angle on the world as the subject-matter of discourse.

Paull Our own dialogue, then, has brought us to **your** hypothesis. My main qualm, however, would be with the global nature of what you are saying. I would like to consider how to apply the idea of point of view to classroom and counselling strategies.

David Yes, I'm sure it would be helpful for both of us if we could keep working until we talked those issues through. At least we have made it possible, through our conversation, to proceed to specific applications. Talk always leads to talk. For instance, the conversation we are having now goes right back to our high school, when one of our teachers talked to me about Vaihinger's *The Philosophy of 'As If'*.

So 17 years after being introduced to that book, we are still building on his talk, his teaching. . .

Paull As well as on the teaching of others before him . . . and since.

Extending the conversation

There are at least two ways in which the argument can be developed. On the one hand, the discourse can be extended to the issues which the dialogue raised but could not treat at length. These include, for example, the analysis of classroom interaction; Bernstein's theory of language codes; the notion of semantic congruence (as it might bear upon the work of Whorf); and the principles which should guide the description of behaviour.

The other way in which the discourse could be developed is more straightforward: namely, by going back to the authorities cited and examining their claims and theories directly. For instance, one might wish to explore Chomsky's view of a universal grammar; or Malinowski's approach to meaning.

Problems and citations
The works cited in this extension are listed at the end.

Since completing the manuscript for this text I have read two essays which could have been given prominence in my own discussion—one paper by the linguist Ruqaiya Hasan, and a book by the educationist Douglas Barnes. Both essays treat issues which the dialogue had to leave underdeveloped. In Ruqaiya Hasan's 'The Ontogenesis of Ideology: An Interpretation of Mother Child Talk', the patterns of mother-child interaction are related to deeply entrenched assumptions in our culture: specifically, the belief that mothers' work is not real work, and the 'silly mummy' syndrome. In making the connection between patterns of talk and ideology, Hasan also presents perhaps the best available clarification of Whorf's theories. Note that an earlier paper by Hasan: 'What Kind of Resource is Language?' is also very helpful, both for its discussion of the nature of language as well as for its observations on mother-child talk and orientation to learning.

Developing the argument

The role of point of view in establishing ways of learning is explored in Douglas Barnes' *From Communication to Curriculum*. Barnes uses a small range of taped lessons in order to argue for the importance of the hypothetical (the as if) mode of classroom discourse. The argument is persuasive; and the general observations on classroom interaction are extremely helpful. The limitations of the book relate mainly to the slight and qualified discussion of linguistic patterns (see for example, pp.69–70).

Without detailed language analysis, Barnes focuses on the hypothetical mode only with students of early secondary school. As I have suggested in the preceding dialogue, a child can be turning her interpersonal meanings into an object of discourse before she is even attending school. The ontogenesis and development of point of view have been wrongly associated, I think, with only older children. (See also C.Atkinson, *Making Sense of Piaget*.)

The discussion of Bernstein's theory of codes can be pursued in the three volume *Class, Codes and Control*. Again, one point of particular clarification is Chapter 10 of Volume 2: Hasan distinguishes between the notions of code, register, and social dialect. Bernstein's work and its implications are also explored throughout M.A.K. Halliday's *Language as Social Semiotic*.

A general view which emerges from the dialogue in this text is that knowledge is constructed through different forms of discourse—knowledge is not simply discovered. The philosophical issues related to constructivism (as well as to the opposing correspondence theories of truth) are clearly presented by Richard Rorty in *Philosophy and the Mirror of Nature,* and *Consequences of Pragmatism*. In the latter book the essay 'Is There a Problem about Fictional Discourse?' should be read first. In a similar vein, Nelson Goodman's *Ways of Worldmaking* is succinct and illuminating. The idea that human beings construct the categories of truth is forcefully presented in Nietzsche's 'On Truth and Falsity in their Extramoral Sense' in W.Shibles, *Essays on Metaphor*.

Exploring the citations

It is to be hoped that most readers will want to read the works of Vygotsky and Luria firsthand. These include: *Thought and Language*, *Cognitive Development: Its Cultural and Social Foundations* and *The Making of Mind: A Personal Account of Soviet Psychology*.

The significance of Wittgenstein's work can be sought in P. M. S. Hacker's study, *Insight and Illusion: Wittgenstein on Philosophy and the Metaphysics of Experience.* There is also the Fontana Modern Masters volume by David Pears, as well as Wittgenstein's own *Philosophical Investigations*. In fact, the various issues that arise from the analytical tradition of philosophy are perhaps best explored through the materials (including audiotapes) prepared by the Open University: (A402) *Thought and Reality: Central Themes in Wittgenstein's Philosophy.* The philosophy of logical atomism might be studied through Bertrand Russell's *An Inquiry into Meaning and Truth; or* John Watling's *Bertrand Russell*.

Chomsky's view of language and mental organs is presented in *Reflections on Language*. A brief, less technical introduction can be found in *Problems of Knowledge and Freedom*.

Studies with interesting methodological implications include C.H.Waddington's *Tools for Thought* and W.Heisenberg's *Physics and Philosophy: The Revolution in Modern Science*. Waddington, a biologist, offers many suggestions concerning the representation of data. He also makes a number of observations on thinghood and the difficulties of treating the process character of experience. Heisenberg's work emphasises the role of the observer, and the limits of empiricism.

The work of Gregory Bateson (e.g. *Mind and Nature: A Necessary Unity*), is relevant to all the issues addressed throughout the dialogue. Bateson is one of the most accomplished inter-disciplinary thinkers of the twentieth century. The following quotation, for instance, explains the significance of an interactionist point of view, an issue Paull emphasised in his references to both teaching and counselling, and an issue which is the foundation of the concept of inter-subjectivity:

> . . . *relationship is always a product of double description.*
>
> It is correct (and a great improvement) to begin to think of the two parties to the interaction as two eyes, each giving a monocular view of what goes on and, together, giving a binocular view in depth. This double view *is* the relationship.
>
> Relationship is not internal to the single person. It is nonsense to talk about 'dependency' or 'aggressiveness' or 'pride', and so on. All such words have their roots in what happens between persons, not in some something-or-other inside a person.

Bateson, p. 146

The citations

Atkinson, C., M*aking Sense of Piaget* (Routledge & Kegan Paul, London, 1983).

Barnes, D. R., *From Communication to Curriculum* (Penguin, Harmondsworth, 1976).

Bateson, G., *Mind and Nature: A Necessary Unity* (Fontana/Collins, Glasgow, 1980).

Bernstein, B., (ed.), *Class, Codes and Control* (Routledge & Kegan Paul, London, 1971–1973–1975).

Chomsky, N., *Reflections on Language* (Pantheon Books, New York, 1975).

Chomsky, N., *Problems of Knowledge and Freedom* (Fontana Collins, Great Britain, 1972).

Goodman, N., *Ways of Worldmaking* (The Harvester Press, Great Britain, 1978).

Hacker, P. M. S., *Insight and Illusion: Wittgenstein on Philosophy and the Metaphysics of Experience* (Oxford University Press, Oxford, 1972).

Halliday, M. A. K., *Language as Social Semiotic* (Edward Arnold, London, 1978).

Hasan, R., 'The ontogenesis of ideology: an interpretation of mother child talk', mimeo.

Hasan, R., 'What kind of resource is language?', *Australian Review of Applied Linguistics*, vol. 7, no. 8, 1984.

Heisenberg, W., *Physics and Philosophy: The Revolution in Modern Science* (Harper and Row, New York, 1962).

Luria, A. R., *Cognitive Development: Its Cultural and Social Foundations*, (ed.) M. Cole (Harvard University Press, USA, 1976).

Luria, A. R., *The Making of Mind: A Personal Account of Soviet Psychology*, (ed.) M. Cole & S. Cole (Harvard University Press, USA, 1979).

Neitzsche, 'On truth and falsity in their extramoral sense', in W. Shibles, *Essays on Metaphor* (Language Press, Wisconsin, 1972).

Open University, (A402) *Thought and Reality: Central Themes in Wittgenstein's Philosophy* (Open University Press, 1976).

Pears, D., *Wittgenstein*, Fontana Modern Masters (Wm. Collins Sons & Co. Ltd, Great Britain, 1971).

Rorty, R., *Philosophy and the Mirror of Nature* (Basil Blackwell, Oxford, 1980).

Rorty, R., *Consequences of Pragmatism* (The Harvester Press, Great Britain, 1982).

Russell, B., *An Inquiry into Meaning and Truth* (Penguin, Harmondsworth, 1973).

Vygotsky, L. S., *Thought and Language* (MIT Press, Massachusetts, 1962).

Waddington, C. H., *Tools for Thought* (Paladin, Herts, 1977).

Watling, J., *Bertrand Russell* (Oliver and Boyd, Edinburgh, 1970).

Wittgenstein, *Philosophical Investigations* (Blackwell, Oxford, 1974).

References

Bateson, G., *Mind and Nature: A Necessary Unity* (Fontana/Collins, Glasgow, 1980).

Black, M., 'Some troubles with Whorfianism', in S. Hook (ed.), *Language and Philosophy* (New York University Press, New York, 1969).

Bohm, D., *Wholeness and the implicate order* (Routledge & Kegan Paul, London, 1980).

Bohr, N., *Atomic Physics and Human Knowledge* (Interscience/John Wiley, New York, 1963).

Carroll, J. B. (ed.), *Language, Thought and Reality* (MIT Press, Massachusetts, 1976).

Chomsky, N., *Reflections on Language* (Pantheon Books, New York, 1975).

Chomsky, N., *Problems of Knowledge and Freedom* (Fontana/Collins, Great Britain, 1972).

Christie, M., *Aboriginal Perspectives on Experience and Learning: The Role of Language in Aboriginal Education*, ECS806 Sociocultural aspects of language and education (Deakin University, Geelong, Victoria, 1985).

Feigl, H., 'Mind-Body, *Not* a Pseudoproblem', in S. Hook (ed.), *Dimensions of Mind* (Collier Books, London, 1961).

Goodman, N., *Ways of Worldmaking* (The Harvester Press, Great Britain, 1978).

Gregory, R. L., *The Intelligent Eye* (McGraw-Hill, New York, 1970).

Halliday, M. A. K. & Hasan, R., *Language, Context, and Text: Aspects of Language in a Social-Semiotic Perspective* (Oxford University Press, Oxford, 1989).

Halliday, M. A. K., *An Introduction to Functional Grammar* (Edward Arnold, London, 1985).

Halliday, M. A. K., *Spoken and Written Language* (Oxford University Press, Oxford, 1989).

Halliday, M. A. K., *Language as Social Semiotic* (Edward Arnold, London, 1978).

Halliday, M. A. K., *Learning How to Mean: Explorations in the Development of Language* (Edward Arnold, London, 1975).

Hasan, R., 'Ways of saying: ways of meaning', in R. P. Fawcett (ed.) et al., *The Semiotics of Culture and Language*, Volume 1, *Language as Social Semiotic* (Frances Pinter, London, 1984).

Hasan, R., *Linguistics, Language, and Verbal Art* (Oxford University Press, Oxford, 1989).

Hasan, R., 'Code, Register and Social Dialect', in B. Bernstein (ed.), *Class, Codes and Control* (Routledge & Kegan Paul, London, 1971-1973-1975).

Heisenberg, W., *Physics and Philosophy* (Harper and Row, New York, 1962).

Hockett, C. F., 'The problem of universals in language', in J. H. Greenberg (ed.), *Universals of Language* (MIT Press, London, 1966).

Jakobson R. & Halle, M., *Fundamentals of Language* (Mouton & Co.'s, Gravenhage, 1956).

Keenan, E. L. & Ochs, Elinor, 'Becoming a competent speaker in Malagasy', in T. Shopen (ed.), *Languages and Their Speakers* (Winthrop Publishers, Massachusetts, 1979).

Koestler, A., *The Ghost in the Machine* (Pan Books, London, 1970).

Lemke, J. L., *Using Language in the Classroom* (Oxford University Press, Oxford, 1989).

Luria, A. R., *Cognitive Development, Its Cultural and Social Foundations*, (ed.) M. Cole (Harvard University Press, USA, 1976).

Luria, A. R., *The Making of Mind: A Personal Account of Soviet Psychology*, (eds.) M. Cole and S. Cole (Harvard University Press, USA, 1979).

Malinowski, B., in C. K. Ogden & I. A. Richards, *The Meaning of Meaning* (Routledge & Kegan Paul, London, 1949).

Marr, D., *Vision*, discussed in I. Rosenfield, 'Seeing through the brain', *New York Review*, Oct. 11, 1984.

Monod, J., *Chance and Necessity* (Collins, Fontana Books, Glasgow, 1974).

Moore, I., *Aktils Big Swim* (Oxford University Press, Melbourne, 1980).

Newson, J., 'The growth of shared understandings between infant and caregiver', in M. Bullowa (ed.), *Before Speech: The Beginning of Interpersonal Communication* (Cambridge University Press, Cambridge, 1979).

O'Toole, L. M., *Structure, Style and Interpretation In the Russian Short Story* (Yale University Press, London, 1982).

Painter, C., *Learning the Mother Tongue* (Oxford University Press, Oxford, 1989).

Popper, K., *Objective Knowledge: An Evolutionary Approach* (Oxford University Press, Great Britain, 1972).

Quine, W. V. O., *From a Logical Point of View* (Harper Torchbooks, New York, 1963).

Rorty, R., *Philosophy and the Mirror of Nature* (Basil Blackwell, Oxford, 1980).

Russell, B., *An Inquiry into Meaning and Truth* (Penguin Books, Harmondsworth, 1973).

de Saussure, F., *Course in General Linguistics,* (ed.) C. Bally & A. Sechehaye in collaboration with A. Riedlinger (Fontana/Collins, Glasgow, 1978).

100

Snell, B., *The Discovery of the Mind: The Greek origins of European thought*, (tr.) T. G. Rosenmeyer (Harper Torchbooks, New York, 1960).

Stevens, W., 'Tattoo' and 'The Load of Sugar-Cane', in *The Collected Poems of Wallace Stevens* (Faber and Faber, London, 1955).

Trevarthen, C., 'Communication and co-operation in early infancy: a description of primary intersubjectivity', in M. Bullowa (ed.), *Before Speech: The Beginning of Interpersonal Communication* (Cambridge University Press, Cambridge, 1979).

Trezise, P. & Roughsey, D., *Turramulli the Giant Quinkin* (Collins, Sydney, 1982).

Vygotsky, L. S., *Thought and Language* (MIT Press, Massachusetts, 1962).

Waddington, C. H., *Tools for Thought* (Paladin, Herts, 1977).

Watling, J., *Bertrand Russell* (Oliver and Boyd, Edinburgh, 1970).

Wheeler, J. A., 'Law without law', in P. Medawar and J. H. Shelley (eds.), *Structure in Science and Art* (Excerpta Medica, Amsterdam, 1980).

Whitehead, A. N., *Process and Reality* (Cambridge University Press, London, 1929).

Wierzbicka, A., *Lingua mentalis: the semantics of natural language* (Academic Press, Sydney, 1980).

Wittgenstein, L., *Tractatus Logico-Philosophicus* (Routledge & Kegan Paul, London, 1974).

Yallop, 'Numerals in Australian Aboriginal Languages', paper given to the Sydney Linguistics Circle, June 1984.

Technical terms

Acknowledgements

Grateful acknowledgement is made to the following sources for material used in this book.

p. 85 'Tattoo'. Copyright 1923 and renewed 1951 by Wallace Stevens. Reprinted from THE COLLECTED POEMS OF WALLACE STEVENS, by Wallace Stevens, by permission of Alfred A. Knopf, Inc. and Faber and Faber Ltd.

p. 86 'The Load of Sugar-Cane'. Copyright 1923, 1951 by Wallace Stevens. Reprinted from THE COLLECTED POEMS OF WALLACE STEVENS, by Wallace Stevens, by permission of Alfred A. Knopf, Inc. and Faber and Faber Ltd.

pp. 39, 40, 41, 42, 43, 45, 46, 47, 50, 65, 66, 93 Extracts from *Cognitive Development* reprinted by permission.

pp. 68, 69, 70 Extracts from *The Discovery of the Mind* reprinted by permission.